The Structure of Medieval Society

LIBRARY OF MEDIEVAL CIVILIZATION
EDITED BY DR JOAN EVANS AND
PROFESSOR CHRISTOPHER BROOKE

CHRISTOPHER BROOKE

The Structure
of Medieval Society

McGRAW-HILL BOOK COMPANY · NEW YORK

Contents

General Editor's Preface

In 1966 a large and handsome book was published by Messrs Thames and Hudson, with the title *The Flowering of the Middle Ages*. The text was provided by a team of scholars under the shrewd and skilful captaincy of Joan Evans, and could be read with pleasure and profit by all those who could afford to buy the book, and had an ample lectern on which to lay it. Word has come to the publishers that there are many who have smaller pockets and less ambitious furniture, who would like none the less to read its chapters as well as to admire the *Flowering*'s illustrations. They therefore asked me to join with Dr Evans in the pleasant task of converting the book into a series of small volumes, each incorporating a chapter of the original. The old chapters have been roused, stretched and shaken into a new and somewhat enlarged shape, have donned their old costume of pictures considerably increased, and now present themselves to the public for inspection. Their enlargement is designed to make them more self-contained, able to walk the world on their own; yet they remain a series none the less, and hope still to walk often in company with one another.

It is with great pleasure that I present to the public my colleagues' books in the Series. As I do so, I recall many kindnesses from many members of Thames and Hudson, and especially from the late Walter Neurath, who inspired the *Flowering*. I give thanks, too, and above all, to Joan Evans, who first enlisted me in *Flowering* and has so readily welcomed and supported my collaboration in this revival and revision.

C.B.

Foreword to the Original Edition

Fifty years ago history was mainly studied in school and university, and as a consequence by the educated reader, in terms of wars, political alliances and constitutional developments. Its base was properly in written documents, and even social history was not envisaged in other than documentary terms. Eight half-tone illustrations were enough for any historical work and most were not illustrated at all.

Now, at least for the general reader, all is changed. Schoolmasters attempt to give some visual background to their history lessons; occasionally even a Professor of History may show a few slides. Professional historians and archivists rightly continue to study every facet of their subject in documented detail, but for most people 'history' has become a much more general matter, that provides them with a background to what they see and what they read. For them, at least, historians must so interpret the documents as to make them reveal the life of the past rather than its battles and its political machinations.

This change is due less to the professional historians themselves than to a change of view in the reading public: a change that can only be paralleled in the second half of the nineteenth century when trains and steamers made it easy to travel and everyone began to know their Europe. That time produced its Ruskin and its Viollet-le-Duc, its Lasteyrie and its Henry Adams; but we forget that Ruskin had to draw, or to engage others to draw for him, the things he wrote and talked about, and that Viollet-le-Duc was never able to reproduce a photograph.

In our own day a new wave of travel by car and plane has been accompanied by incredible developments in photography and in reproduction. Black and white photographs and half-tone blocks revolutionized the study of architecture and art at the end of the nineteenth century, and the great archaeological discoveries of the day made the general public willing to accept an object or a building *pari passu* with a written document. In our own time colour photographs and colour plates have enriched these studies in a way that would have seemed miraculous to Ruskin.

Moreover, though education remains astonishingly bookish, our recreations have trained our eyes. An experienced and successful lecturer of 1900 said that a slide must remain on the screen for at least a minute to give the audience time to take it in. Now, the cinema screen and the television set have trained us in visual nimbleness, and we 'see' much more quickly. . . .

Somewhere about 1100 it seems as if Europe settled on an even keel. In England the Norman dynasty had established itself militarily and administratively. In France Philip I had established a rival kingdom, the Cluniac reform had revivified religious life, and the Crusades had started on their way. In Germany Henry IV was establishing the Empire on a firmer basis. In Italy Pope Gregory VII had lost his fight against the Emperor, but had gained new spiritual force for Rome. In Spain Alfonso VI of Castile had made Toledo the capital of Christian Spain, and the Cid had conquered Valencia. In the Eastern Empire the Comneni had suffered the inroads first of the Normans and then of the Crusaders; the weight of power was shifting westward. In Europe it is fair to say that a measure of stability had been achieved, in which the forces of feudalism, monasticism, scholastic philosophy and civic growth could work together to make the history of the Middle Ages.

To make that history more real to the ordinary reader is our purpose. The authors have not here published unknown documents, unknown monuments or unknown works of art, but have tried by the interpretation of what is known to make the Christian civilization of Europe in the Middle Ages more significant and more comprehensible to the readers of today. The keyword to our conception of history is civilization.

JOAN EVANS

Chapter One

Introduction

Medieval society was hierarchical: to the distant and super- *1*
ficial view, its structure was clear and firm. A brief introduction to the social structure of medieval western Europe
must therefore sketch this hierarchy. It is not, however, the
purpose of this book to draw a formal picture of a social
ladder, but rather to trace a pattern in which the formal
hierarchy, its props and supports, is clearly and concretely
linked with some of the criticisms, deviations, exceptions and
absurdities which, like all formal social structures, it was
compelled to tolerate. The critics included heretics and
dissenters; but also some of the pillars of the Catholic Church
and of the social hierarchy. For at its heart lay a paradox: one
of the chief supports of social hierarchy was the Christian
Church, also dedicated to the view, and constantly asserting,
that in the eyes of God all men are equal; worshipping a God
who was no respecter of persons, and was thought to be not
at all disinclined, as was emphasized in countless medieval
paintings and sculptures, to assign popes and kings to hell. *5*
    No attempt could possibly be made in so brief a space to
give a comprehensive picture of any aspect of medieval
society; what is attempted is a series of interlocking examples
of topics and themes, which are intended to cohere with one
another and to reveal the interplay of formal hierarchy and
exception, of defence and criticism, of government, organization and anarchy. Yet behind all this lay a deeply and widely
felt acceptance of hierarchy, of social degree, which lasted
for many centuries longer than those of this book; and was
reckoned to be so inherent in God's creation that not only
society, but the whole structure of the universe reflected it.

Its most famous expression is in the words put into the mouth of Ulysses in Shakespeare's *Troilus and Cressida*.

> *The heavens themselves, the planets, and this centre*
> *Observe degree, priority, and place,*
> *Insisture, course, proportion, season, form,*
> *Office, and custom, in all line of order:*
> *And therefore is the glorious planet Sol*
> *In noble eminence enthron'd and spher'd*
> *Amidst the other; whose med'cinable eye*
> *Corrects the ill aspects of planets evil,*
> *And posts, like the commandment of a king,*
> *Sans check, to good and bad: but when the planets*
> *In evil mixture to disorder wander,*
> *What plagues, and what portents, what mutiny,*
> *What raging of the sea, shaking of earth,*
> *Commotion in the winds, frights, changes, horrors,*
> *Divert, and crack, rend and deracinate*
> *The unity and married calm of states*
> *Quite from their fixture! O! when degree is shak'd,*
> *Which is the ladder to all high designs,*
> *The enterprise is sick. How could communities,*
> *Degrees in schools, and brotherhoods in cities,*
> *Peaceful commerce from dividable shores,*
> *The primogenitive and due of birth,*
> *Prerogative of age, crowns, sceptres, laurels,*
> *But by degree, stand in authentic place?*
> *Take but degree away, untune that string,*
> *And, hark! what discord follows; each thing meets*
> *In mere oppugnancy: the bounded waters*
> *Should lift their bosoms higher than the shores,*
> *And make a sop of all this solid globe:*
> *Strength should be lord of imbecility,*
> *And the rude son should strike his father dead:*
> *Force should be right; or rather, right and wrong –*
> *Between whose endless jar justice resides –*
> *Should lose their names, and so should justice too.*

1   The hierarchy of powers. In this fresco by Andrea da Firenze in the Spanish Chapel in Santa Maria Novella, at Florence, the spiritual and temporal hierarchies – pope, cardinal, bishop, abbot, clergy; emperor, count palatine, gentlemen, peasants and pilgrims – are shown in their relation to the Dominican friars, for whom the fresco was painted in 1355. The Dominicans are shown not only as human friars, in black and white habit, in a group with other religious, but also as *Domini canes*, 'hounds of the Lord', protecting the Christian flock against heretic wolves

Then every thing includes itself in power,
Power into will, will into appetite;
And appetite, a universal wolf,
So doubly seconded with will and power,
Must make perforce a universal prey,
And last, eat up himself.

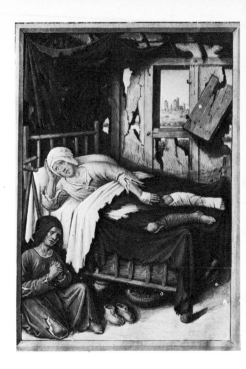

2–4 Scenes of family life, from a French miniature of *c*. 1490. The theme is four states of society, of which three are shown here. The first shows husband and wife in a peasant's hovel; next, in a carpenter's shop – with the craftsman at work, his wife spinning, a boy at her feet; the last, a family tableau from a rich man's household. These are scenes from the end of the Middle Ages, and the furniture is more elaborate (though not necessarily more comfortable) than in the twelfth or thirteenth centuries

In other words, Troy would have fallen long ago, Ulysses believes, if proper respect for rank and dignity had been observed among the Greeks. It was appreciated that Ulysses had been a pagan, and so there is nothing specifically Christian in his sentiments; yet there is nothing to which the majority of medieval Catholics would have objected; quite the contrary. Virtually all orthodox Catholics who reflected seriously on such matters regarded the hierarchy of medieval society as having divine sanction; even if government and authority might in some measure, or in some men's view, be the result of the Fall. Hierarchy was an essential element in the world they knew, not just a man-made thing; and to the medieval Catholic it was a hierarchy in which divine and human, living and dead, were inextricably mingled. St-Denis was the Westminster Abbey of the French kings; and we shall see that a French king could act as St Denis's vassal exactly as if he were a living man, save only that his status as

a patron saint made him (what no ordinary mortal could have been) the king's superior. In Westminster Abbey itself *28–30*
one cannot fail to be struck by the way in which the tombs of the English kings cluster round their patron saint, Edward the Confessor, itself set immediately behind the high altar. Thus, symbolically, three vital elements in the social hierarchy, God, a saint and the king, are juxtaposed.

Under God and the saints, the hierarchy consisted of two *1*
ladders: a spiritual hierarchy with the pope, bishops, abbots, monks, canons and friars on its higher rungs; and a secular ladder, topped by kings, princes, nobles, barons and knights, and well-to-do burgesses. On the lower rungs were set the rank and file of clergy and laity, the parish priests and lesser folk on the one side, the peasants and lesser artisans on the other. The relations between the two ladders were never simple. A bishop, as a spiritual pastor, was independent of the *6*
secular ladder; he was also, commonly, the subject of a king.

A peasant, in principle, might become pope. It almost never happened; but it was undoubtedly much easier for a man of ability, who attracted the right kind of patronage, to move great distances up the spiritual ladder. Social position depended on status and office more than on birth; but birth, needless to say, always counted too, especially in the later Middle Ages, and this relation between the spiritual and secular ladders created a series of barriers, misunderstandings and snobberies crude and subtle, which were in some places and in some measure counteracted by the nature of the spiritual hierarchy. Thus behind the clear, even simple, façade lay a series of subtle gradations, frictions and paradoxes, which lend a special difficulty, and a special fascination, to the study of medieval society.

5   The mouth of hell, a detail from a Last Judgment painted by Stefan Lochner *c.* 1430–50. A terrified group, including a king, a bishop, a cardinal and a pope, is pulled into the deepest abyss

6   The feast of relics, from a fifteenth-century breviary. The picture shows the office in progress on the feast; pilgrims visit relics laid on an altar on the left; bishops venerate a shrine on the right; a preacher expounds their merits at the foot. It illustrates a prayer asking that 'the merits of Holy Mary, Mother of God and ever Virgin, and of the saints whose relics are contained in this Church, may protect us.' Folk from every walk of life are shown paying their respects to the heavenly hierarchy

mie. justi in perpetui. Scor
mentis.
... erunum in dno. fulgebut iusti
& tanqm scintille in arundineto discur
rent iudicabunt naciones & nacra
bunt ineternum. Magnificat.

Presta quesumus
omnipotens deus
ut sancte dei geni
tris semper uirginis marie
& sanctor tuor quor relq̄e
in hac continentur ecclesia
nos protegant merita quatm

Chapter Two

The Pope and the Beggar

7 In the summer of 1210 a ragged band of a dozen beggars waited on the greatest potentate in Christendom, Pope Innocent III. They demanded permission to live according to a religious Rule which committed them to obedience and chastity and a poverty more total than any officially accepted Rule had hitherto enforced. They won from the Pope some measure of verbal approval. The Pope had been prepared for this concession by a dream, if the story made famous by Giotto's fresco in the Upper Church at Assisi is true: the

8 Lateran Palace, the headquarters of the papacy since the days of the Emperor Constantine, was falling down, and was saved from destruction by a poor, despised beggar.

The contrast of rich and poor in this story struck contemporaries as it strikes us. We are not unfamiliar with the problems of want and poverty; but our attitude is fundamentally different from that of St Francis and Pope Innocent, because we no longer accept poverty as an inevitable part of the order of things. An affluent society can contemplate the abolition of poverty, at least as a conceivable ideal. In an underdeveloped or developing society, like those of western Europe in the Middle Ages, full employment is impossible and a high proportion of the population must resign themselves to seasonal employment – to long hours of labour at time of harvest or when the retinue of a great man has to be transported through their villages, to long hours of idleness in winter, and perhaps to famine if the harvest is poor. Many people had their plots of land to till; for them poverty meant a low standard of living and something worse in a bad year. Many more were landless, and for these poverty could be a

7   St Francis presents his Rule to Pope Innocent III, in 1210, from the fresco attributed to Giotto in the Upper Church at Assisi. 'And in few words and simply I had it written down, and the Lord Pope confirmed it to me . . .' (see p. 130)

harsher and more constant companion. All had their compensations: the need for mutual aid is a natural assumption in such societies, and the Church constantly preached to the wealthy their duty to be generous in charity to the poor and provided at least a theoretical framework of poor relief.

8–10　The story of St Francis in art. *Below:* the Pope's dream, from the fresco attributed to Giotto in the Upper Church at Assisi. Innocent III dreams that the Lateran Palace is falling, and is saved by St Francis. *Right:* St Francis of Assisi, from the fresco attributed to Cimabue in the Lower Church at Assisi, of the late thirteenth century. This is the most remarkable of the early pictures of Francis, but as it was painted two generations after his death it is most unlikely to be based on any recollection of what he really looked like. *Below right:* St Francis cuts out his habit of coarse cloth – 'Seint Fraunceis taille sun abite de meynel'. English, *c.* 1325

11–14 The beggars. *Right:* St Martin sharing his cloak with a beggar. English, *c.* 1280. *Opposite:* sick beggars – a leper with a begging bowl, a cripple on crutches, French, fourteenth century, and a leper woman with a bell – 'sum good my gentyll mayster for God sake', English, fourteenth century. *Opposite below,* the parable of Dives and Lazarus from the porch at Moissac, *c.* 1125–30: on the right Dives fares sumptuously, while on the left dogs lick Lazarus's sores and an angel prepares to carry his soul to Abraham's bosom

11–13 Under these conditions it is understandable that poverty should be taken for granted – 'the poor you have always with you'. We are often tempted to think that this acceptance was too easy: to suggest, for example, that it would have been better to pay higher wages than for so many folk to depend on charity and largesse. This is in part because we are not accustomed to the workings of such societies, though many similar ones exist in the world today. In practice higher wages would often have meant that fewer men were employed, that more were totally unemployed; and for many the hope of lavish charity was the only barrier between them

and the threat of disaster. In a similar way the tendency of
medieval churchmen to idealize poverty jars on the modern
student. There was indeed little that was sentimental in this:
the story of Dives and Lazarus, the constant source of hope
for the Christian poor, paints a picture of Lazarus's sufferings
in this world which was harsh and vivid and true to the
experience of medieval life. Poverty was a constant and tragic
fact of experience; one of the great problems of the Church
was to make the facts of life palatable while alleviating their
consequences.

14

15 The rich man's hope. St Peter receives the Duc de Berry at the gate of heaven, with the respect due to his rank. From the *Grandes Heures du duc de Berry*, 1409

Wealth, Charity and Hopes of Heaven

Nor was the lot of the rich entirely enviable. Wealth was insecure; disaster could come swiftly and unforeseen, and churchmen were inclined to find it their duty from time to time to remind their hearers that 'it is easier for a camel to go through the eye of a needle, than for a rich man to enter into the kingdom of God'. There was indeed, on this as on every topic, much diversity of view; but in most men's eyes the force of this text was mitigated by two circumstances. First of all, particularly in the early Middle Ages, it was reckoned that in any case very few would be saved – Lazarus was almost as sure of torment as Dives. From the twelfth century onwards the prospects of mankind in the after-life brightened, at the same time as they were brightening in the present; and the social value of wealth, as well as its traditional secular enjoyment, was too engrained for the fate of Dives constantly to disturb the rich man's sleep. It was appreciated in any case that the saying of Jesus was related essentially to what a man did with his wealth; and it was universally assumed in theory at least that a man's resources were a trust of which he was the steward rather than the owner. So long as a man spent lavishly on charity – used his money and did not hoard it – the Church was happy. A diplomatic English bishop of the twelfth century could write a letter to a great and wealthy earl, in which he slipped in a reference to the needle's eye merely as prelude to commending the earl for his large and systematic almsgiving, and other pious works.

The real sin, in medieval eyes, was avarice, and its close *16* companion, usury. Money was there to be spent, not to be hoarded or invested. The Church preached charity, the world preached lavish display and splendid hospitality; a good man was expected to live beyond his income. With certain differences and qualifications, this applied to churchmen as well as to laymen. At its crudèst, display could be

16 Avarice. The miser still grips his money bags while the devil prepares to carry him off – from an eleventh-twelfth-century capital in the Nièvre

25

17 The Carceri. This small convent, revived in the fifteenth century, marks the
site of a favourite retreat of St Francis and his companions, on the slopes of
Monte Subasio above Assisi. Hidden in the woods and rocks are the cells and
caves of the early friars

taken as a sign of divine favour. The heathen of Pomerania in the early twelfth century repudiated a group of ascetic missionaries who came to preach the Gospel in rags; but chased each other into the baptistery when they saw the splendid vestments and magnificent retinue of Bishop Otto of Bamberg; nor were there lacking men in Christendom itself who took the wealth and outward show of the Church to be a sign of divine favour. Most men assumed that the rich and powerful lived up to their wealth; and although Rome's love of gold was a constant and favourite theme with satirists from the eleventh century onwards, it was normally taken for granted that the princes of the Church should live surrounded by magnificence. When Francis appeared before Pope Innocent in rags, he meant no criticism of the Pope: his life and writings reveal at every turn implicit acceptance and respect for the papacy as he knew it, in an age in which pope and Curia had many critics. The world had its palaces and its hovels; and the Church, as Francis saw it, must to this extent be the mirror of the world, in that it too had its princes and its beggars.

'In one of the frescoes of the Upper Church of Assisi', wrote Paul Sabatier in his *Life of St Francis of Assisi*, 'Giotto has represented St Clare and her companions coming out from S. Damiano all in tears, to kiss their spiritual father's corpse as it is being carried to its last home. With an artist's liberty he has made the chapel a rich church built of precious marbles. *19*

'Happily the real S. Damiano is still there, nestled under *18* some olive-trees like a lark under the heather; it still has its ill-made walls of irregular stones, like those which bound the neighbouring fields. Which is the more beautiful, the ideal temple of the artist's fancy, or the poor chapel of reality? No heart will be in doubt.'

The decoration of churches offers a different, but not wholly dissimilar contrast to that between the way of life of beggars and princes. In the early twelfth century there arose the heresy of the Petrobrusians, who in many respects

18, 19 San Damiano, Assisi – 'the poor chapel of reality' (*left*) and 'the ideal temple of the artist's fancy', the fresco in the Upper Church at Assisi showing St Clare and her companions coming out in tears to kiss St Francis's body

anticipated the doctrines of the more puritanical of the Protestant Reformers. They disapproved of richly ornate churches root and branch, and put their disapproval to practical effect by sacking churches and making bonfires of crucifixes. The attack on ornament was not confined to the unorthodox. No one was stricter in Catholic orthodoxy in the age of the Petrobrusians than St Bernard of Clairvaux; yet in a famous diatribe Bernard lavished all the arts of Latin rhetoric on a denunciation of the glories of the abbey of Cluny in his day. Clairvaux – and all the churches of the Cistercian Order while Bernard lived and reigned – had bare walls, windows of plain glass, wooden altars: no images, no stained glass windows, no wall-paintings, no silver or gold or precious stones; all these were regarded as distractions. The minds of the monks must be turned away from earthly glories to those of heaven. This view was doubtless accepted by Bernard's very numerous followers; but there were many more in the same age who believed the exact opposite. Thus Abbot Suger, in one of the books in which he described his labours for his abbey of St-Denis, near Paris, openly and directly defended the opposite opinion. He described 'the increase which almighty God of His beneficence had granted to this church in the time of our prelacy, both in the acquisition of new lands and in the recovery of what had

20, 21

22

20, 21 Cluniac and Cistercian. An eighteenth-century watercolour of the third church at Cluny, 1086–1121, and *below*, beasts of the kind St Bernard denounced on the splendid early twelfth-century tympanum at Beaulieu

22 In contrast, the bare simplicity of Fontenay, a perfect Cistercian church of the mid-twelfth century, originally provided with simple furniture and white-washed walls, otherwise much as now

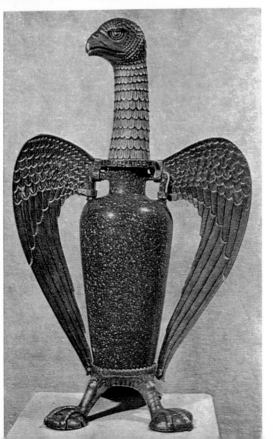

23–25 Abbot Suger, *Sugerius abbas*, and two of the ornaments which he acquired and described so lovingly. The picture above shows the abbot, prostrate at the feet of the Blessed Virgin, in a stained glass window at St-Denis, the abbey which he entered as a boy and served all his life. *Left:* 'We adapted for the service of the altar, with the aid of gold and silver, a porphyry vase, made admirable by the hand of the sculptor and polisher, after it had lain idly in a chest for many years, converting it from a flagon into the shape of an eagle.' *Right:* 'We also procured for the services at the . . . altar a precious chalice out of one solid sardonyx'

been lost . . . in the construction of buildings and in the gathering of gold, silver and most precious jewels and splendid tapestries'. We are given a vivid impression of the aging abbot contemplating with complacent affection the glories of the church he had done so much to beautify, and *23–25* dwelling with particular delight on the precious stones in the great cross and reliquaries on and above the high altar. He quoted the prophet Ezekiel: 'Every precious stone was thy covering, the sardius, the topaz, and the jasper, the chrysolite,

and the onyx, and the beryl, the sapphire, and the carbuncle, and the emerald.' He noted with satisfaction that all these stones were there, save only the carbuncle, and then went on to describe how contemplation of their earthly beauty drew his mind away from the cares of the world to contemplate the heavenly virtues which the jewels represented; how they helped directly to transport his mind to a higher world. And he argued that the most precious and expensive things should be used for the administration of the Holy Eucharist. Those who take a different view object that a 'holy, pure mind and faithful intention' are what count; these are of first importance, admits Suger, but 'we assert that we should do service in the outward ornaments of the vessels we use' as well as in purity of heart.

Chapter Three

Kings and Kingship

Suger was a business man and a man of taste as well as an abbot, and it will not have escaped notice how closely he associates the economic improvement of his abbey's properties – as he would have said, the properties of Denis, patron saint of his abbey and of the kingdom of France – with the adornment of the church. He was several other things besides: author, diplomat and statesman. Francis and Innocent have served to illustrate some of the fundamental social contrasts in the Church and the world in the Middle Ages; Suger and his jewels may now serve to draw our minds to the range of interests which a monk-statesman could have, and so to some of the contrasts in medieval government.

Abbot Suger was a man of exceptional talent. It perhaps seems strange to us today that the interests and experience of a medieval monk should fit him to rule a kingdom; yet Suger was one of the leading statesmen of France and effective ruler of the French kingdom in the late 1140s, when King Louis VII (1137–80) was absent on the Second Crusade. Any abbot had in some degree the responsibilities of a landowner, but the Cistercians tried to combine these with as complete a withdrawal from the world as was feasible. This was in part a deliberate reaction from the involvement of the old Benedictine houses in secular affairs. The monks of St-Denis lived in their cloister and worshipped in the abbey choir, both of them, in the main, reserved to their sole use. Yet the abbey was in some ways very much in the world. The nave of the abbey church was open to laymen and women, who came in throngs as pilgrims on the festivals of St Denis; one of Suger's motives in rebuilding was to give these throngs

26 Abbot Suger's ambulatory at St-Denis, the cradle of Gothic: the space behind the High Altar and the tomb of St Denis

27 One of the altars at St-Denis as it appeared in the fifteenth century, with one of Suger's retables, and his Cross of St Eloi, portrayed in *The Mass of St Giles* of *c.* 1495 in the National Gallery, London

more space and to open the church's vistas, so that pilgrims could admire and enjoy its beauties and look through the choir to the high altar and the reliquaries.

The domain over which the French kings had effective control between the establishment of the dynasty of Hugh Capet in 987 and the end of the twelfth century was narrow; and the result was that they wandered less and had a more stable headquarters than the English kings of the same period. Thus Paris, long the greatest city of the kingdom, was the undisputed capital of the French kings. For centuries kings and abbots had co-operated to tighten the knots which attached the abbey to the monarchy and to spread the cult of St Denis, patron of both. When Suger had finished his work pilgrims from all over the kingdom could look up the

vista to the apse, and in the apse, between altar and vault, 26
surrounded by the ornaments which sparkled with Suger's
favourite jewels, see the shrine of St Denis; and before and 27
behind lay the tombs of Frankish kings of every century from
the sixth to their own.

28–30 The royal tombs in Westminster Abbey. *Left:* the shrine of St Edward the Confessor, behind the High Altar, much restored, but in its original situation, as it was planned by Henry III, 1216–72, to be the centre of the design and vista in his new abbey church. This view looks east, past the tombs of Richard II, Edward III (*bottom*) and Queen Philippa to the chapel of Henry V; round the north side are Henry III (*below*) and Edward I

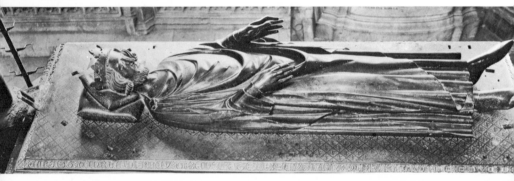

Down to the mid-eleventh century the English kings had no capital like Paris, no patron saint, and no mausoleum comparable with St-Denis. The chief seat of government lay perhaps in Winchester; the leading city of the kingdom was London. It was no doubt in direct imitation of St-Denis that Edward the Confessor (1042–66) revived and substantially enlarged Westminster Abbey and made it for the English kings what St-Denis was for the French. Like St-Denis it collected royal tombs, and, also like St-Denis, it fabricated legends and privileges, so that it presently became established that a king must be anointed and crowned in the abbey. In the mid-twelfth century the monks of Westminster successfully petitioned the Pope for Edward's canonization, and his shrine assumed the place in the abbey that the shrine of Denis occupied in the French abbey, though Edward never became a national patron saint. In the mid-thirteenth century King Henry III, like Suger a great connoisseur, though, unlike Suger, no statesman, dedicated his best energies to rebuilding the abbey to the honour of God, the English monarchy and Edward the Confessor; and he showed his devotion to one source of English royal legend by calling his eldest son Edward, just as Henry VII was to show his interest in another by calling his eldest son Arthur. The ranks of royal tombs *28–30* from the chapel of King Edward to the chapel of King Henry VII in Westminster Abbey today are the result of this fostering of the links of king and abbey in imitation of the French kings and St-Denis.

Portrait of Louis VI

In his later years, Suger was given to reminiscence; and the young monks of the abbey, who had often stayed up late out of respect for his 'narrative old age', urged him to put on parchment the account of his administration of the abbey. He also took time off to write an account of the reign of his first royal patron, King Louis VI (1108–37). A king could not live by legends alone. Of this Suger was well aware. He knew

31 The seal of the City of London, thirteenth century. St Paul, as the patron of the Cathedral (and, with St Thomas Becket, one of the patrons of the City) presides over London, represented by a gate, walls and some of its many towers and spires

32 The ceremony of anointing and coronation. This early fourteenth-century miniature, probably French, shows the final stage, the king enthroned, with orb and sceptre; the vessels held by his shoulders carried the holy oil for the earlier anointing

how important were such things as strategy and finance. The point may be illustrated by looking for a moment at London. It was not Westminster Abbey which made London the capital of England: already the greatest city, its position at the centre of communications in the south-east of the country when England was ruled (as it had been in Roman times) by a dynasty whose older established interests lay on the Continent, made it a natural centre of government in the twelfth and thirteenth centuries when government was growing more stable and administration coming to need (for the first time in the Middle Ages) a permanent headquarters. The arrival of London as a capital is marked, not by the revival of the abbey in the eleventh century, still less by the establishment of Parliament, which could meet in Oxford as late as 1681, but by the final establishment of the royal treasury there in the late twelfth century.

Suger's *Life of Louis VI* is full of wars and rumours of wars. Louis was a strenuous, conscientious and chivalrous man, and none of these qualities lost anything in the telling. His summers were filled with warfare, especially with efforts to repress lawlessness and piracy by the disobedient lords of his own domain. He also found time for the personal exercise of royal justice; and his justice was widely admired, so that the

super infernu̅ ⁊ co̅tuibat̅ ē̅ nalde ⁊
laxate sunt o̅s a̅i̅e q̅ erant i̅ inferno ⁊
clama̅la̅t noce magna dice̅tes b̅n̅
dicim̅us te r̅e̅ si̅u de̅i mu̅ q̅ dignat̅

es nob̅ir fugere̅ ui̅ dat̅ l̅j̅ dici ⁊ b̅j̅ nor̅
tis quam totum te̅r̅p̅ q̅ um̅im̅us
t̅r̅ tu̅a̅. ui ergo qui tui̅co duit dic̅ i̅d̅r̅a̅
qui̅ n̅p̅i h̅e̅b̅ir̅t̅ p̅r̅e̅ a̅i̅ sc̅as̅ i̅ sc̅a̅ sc̅lo̅r̅.

33, 34 King-making. *Above:* the anointing and coronation of Edward the Confessor. A disciple's copy of a drawing by his master, Matthew Paris, the famous St Albans monk, historian and artist. *Below:* the coronation chair of 1300 in Westminster Abbey, with the Stone of Scone, symbol of Scottish kingship, beneath it

35 The Holy Lance, an imperial talisman of great age, carried before the Emperor Otto the Great at the battle of Lechfeld in 955 and still preserved with other imperial insignia at Vienna

semi-independent princes (dukes and counts) who ruled the rest of France occasionally submitted their disputes to him. But on the whole he was one among a group of princes, in most of his affairs no more than *primus inter pares*. Yet he held in reserve the legend of a great past and he was an anointed king. He was successor to Charlemagne, who had ruled over most of western Europe. The other princes of France, in some measure, acknowledged that he was their feudal overlord. Against a king you could rebel, if you thought your cause just (as rebels easily do); but in some sense it was widely thought impossible, or very difficult, to wash the balm from an anointed king; and it was very unusual for a king to be deposed or to die a violent death. The feudal bond, the traditional aura of kingship and pious legend had their uses; and this too was well known to Suger. In 1124 he was able to act as stage manager to a little drama.

32–34

Henry V, King of Germany and, like nearly all the kings of Germany of these centuries, Holy Roman Emperor, formed an alliance with Henry I, King of England and Duke of Normandy, who as Duke was formally a vassal of Louis, and as father of the Empress Matilda was father-in-law to the Emperor. The Emperor Henry V put a large army into the field and made a sudden attack on Rheims.

'When King Louis had received reports from his friends of this attack, he vigorously and boldly set in motion a levy which he had not looked to hold, gathered his nobles and explained what was afoot. He knew from many folks' report and his own frequent experience that St Denis is the special patron and unique protector after God of the kingdom. So he hastened to him, and urged him from his heart, with prayers and gifts, to defend the kingdom, preserve his person, and resist his enemies as was his custom. The blessed and wondrous defender and his companions [i.e. their relics] . . . if another kingdom dares invade the kingdom of the French, are placed on Denis's altar to conduct the defence; and so this was done with splendour and devotion in the King's presence.

43

Then the King took from the altar the standard [the Ori-flamme] of the county of the Vexin – as Count, Louis was a vassal of the Church; he took it under oath as from his over-lord; and he flew against the enemy with a small force on his own account, strongly urging the whole of France to follow him. The accustomed ardour of France was roused by the unaccustomed audacity of her enemies; it spread everywhere and gathered a military levy, a strong force of men, their minds full of ancient courage and former victories.'

The combined generalship of king and relics proved irre-sistible. Levies came to Rheims from many parts of northern France. The Duke of Aquitaine made a gesture of interest. The Count of Blois, nephew to the King of England and his ally, and so officially at war with Louis, appeared in person to join his host. The German army melted rapidly away, and Louis returned to Paris in triumph.

'During all the time of the host's gathering the silver caskets, holy and venerable, containing the most holy relics, lay on the high altar. The monks celebrated office there con-stantly day and night, and flocks of devoted people and pious women came to pray for the army. And so [on his return] the pious King with filial devotion and copious tears, on his own shoulders carried his lords and patrons back to their place, and rewarded them for these and other good works with numerous gifts of land and other benefits.'

Earthly Crowns: the Secular Monarch

It is a nice point whether the relics of Denis, memory of their feudal oaths or common interest had more effect on the princes who assembled at Rheims to confound the invader; but each in its way played its part, and the effect was a notable victory for the one of the three kings whom any ordinary calculation would have reckoned the least powerful. The Emperor's invasion was part of a strategy concerted with his father-in-law, Henry I of England. Henry of England attri-buted the débâcle to the inadequacy of the Emperor's army

36   The Imperial Crown of Otto I, 936–73, still preserved among the imperial
insignia in Vienna. The plates and cross are Byzantine work of the tenth century;
the bow was added in the time of Conrad II, 1024–39; beneath it sat the cloth cap,
the *mitra*, symbol of the Emperor's spiritual authority

and its method of recruitment, and he advised his son-in-law
to levy a tax and hire mercenaries, over whom he would
have more control than over the levies from his domains
and those of his bishops and leading nobles, who came to his
banner according to a traditional contract, none too well
defined. But the German kingdom, though the largest and
traditionally the most powerful in western Europe, was comparatively poor in economic resources, and Henry V lacked

the freedom of manœuvre of his father-in-law. Henry I of England was a man of the world, which helps to explain why he was successful in some of his endeavours, and unsuccessful in his wars against Louis VI. His father, William the Conqueror, had ruled Normandy by inheritance, England, whatever he might claim, by conquest; and he had made his conquest effective by building royal castles, by using the financial and administrative resources of the kingdom to the full, and by developing the bonds which linked him to his leading subjects, the 'feudal' bonds as they are commonly called. He developed the doctrine that great barons and bishops held all their lands of him, in return for military service. He and his successors recruited their armies of *38–40* 'knights' and archers by a judicious mixture of laying out money on mercenaries and of exploiting their subjects' obligation to serve. Yet there was much more in the bonds of king and barons than this. The barons swore oaths to the king and thereby became his personal followers; and all the Conqueror's barons owed their possessions in England to his personal patronage. So large and successful a conquest can happen only at rare intervals, and Henry I had to deal with a baronage which owed nothing to him. The Conqueror's eldest son inherited Normandy; William, the second son, became King of England; and it was only when William was killed in the New Forest in August 1100, that Henry could take any substantial part of his father's inheritance. He claimed England by inheritance, and in 1106 took Normandy by conquest, consigning his eldest brother to prison for life. Whenever opportunity offered he formed new baronies, raised new barons who would owe their wealth and power to him and not to his father or one of his brothers, and so by an extensive use of patronage made his court what his father's had been, a personal reflection of the reigning king's glory. Castles, *42–43* knights, archers, landed wealth, silver coins, and the personal bonds and relations which tied the barons to him and kept them loyal – these were the pillars of Henry I's strength.

37 *Above:* a king's nightmare. Henry I of England, 1100–35, dreams that he is threatened by the three orders of the kingdom, peasants, knights and barons, and bishops and abbots. From the contemporary chronicle of John of Worcester

38–40 Three knights. *Top left:* an aquamanile, a vessel from which water was poured between courses at a feast to wash the hands of the guests, *c.* 1300. *Centre:* a relief of an armed knight, probably twelfth century, from the church of Notre Dame de la Règle, Limoges. *Bottom:* an archer, in knight's armour, in the Bayeux Tapestry, late eleventh century. He shows how important archers were in the Norman army

41 Papal monarchy. Boniface VIII, 1294–1303, presides over a consistory, from a late fourteenth-century manuscript of his Sext (Liber Sextus of the Decretals), with coats of arms of late fourteenth-century cardinals

In different proportions all these items figured in the list of properties of the monarchies of the genial Louis VI of France and the ruthless Emperor Henry V. Both had less command of money; and so both were more dependent on their relations with their subjects to recruit their armies. In Louis's case these relations were close only with the lands and men of his own royal domain, the Ile de France; Henry's domains were wider, and he exercised more control over the dukes, archbishops and bishops of Germany at large than Louis could command outside the Ile de France. But the dukes were not Henry's creations, nor did they owe him precisely defined services; and in his later years one of the greatest of them, Lothar of Saxony, held wholly aloof. Earls who held aloof from the court of Henry I were liable to find themselves rapidly extinguished.

42 The earliest medieval account: the Pipe Roll of Henry I, 1130. This is the audit of the sheriffs' accounts. The extract lists a series of barons' debts to the king

43 Silver and gold coins. From left to right, silver pennies of William I (obverse above, reverse below), and Henry III (short cross and long cross types), and a gold penny of Henry III (all slightly enlarged). The gold penny was not a success, and down to the fourteenth century almost all payments like those given in the Pipe Roll opposite as l.s.d.m. (£, shillings, pence, marks – 1 m. = 13s. 4d.) were actually paid in silver pennies

Louis VI had, nonetheless, some remarkable successes, although he was a man of mediocre resources and very ordinary attainments. These he owed to strenuous activity (sustained till very near the end of his life, when obesity and illness finally made it impossible for him to be lifted into the saddle), to good fortune, to the fact that he was the kind of man who was implicitly trusted, and to his good relations with the Church. The eleventh century had witnessed a dramatic transformation in the papacy, followed by the creation of the papal monarchy: the attempt to make actual in the life of Christendom the papacy's ancient claims to primacy and leadership. One pillar of this was the·attempt to reduce lay influence in the appointment of bishops, an influence particularly symbolized by the act of investiture, by which the king presented a new bishop with ring and pastoral

49

staff, which were commonly reckoned the spiritual symbols of his office. In the opening years of the twelfth century the kings of England, France and Germany were all in different ways trying to defend themselves against the popes' condemnation of this practice. Their methods were characteristic of the men. Louis VI, who was effective ruler even before his father's death in 1108, had influence over a narrow circle of bishoprics outside his domain, and was fearful of losing it; and he had little understanding of the newfangled papal pretensions. But he was a pious man and in no position to resist strong pressure; in due course he began to understand a little of the papacy's views, and rather more of the value of its alliance to him; and in later years the influence of Suger and St Bernard made his relations with Church and papacy close, greatly to the practical benefit of both parties. Henry I of England carried his defence of lay investiture to the point of an open breach with his archbishop, St Anselm, and the Pope. But Henry needed all the support he could get for the conquest of Normandy; and once he had grasped that he could surrender the ceremony of investiture while retaining control over appointments, the way was open for the compromise negotiated in 1106–7. The Emperor Henry V tried to enforce his will by violence: he captured the Pope and extracted a full concession from him, a concession that the Pope was bound to repudiate as soon as the Alps divided him from Henry. The Emperor's violence only embittered the dispute and uselessly prolonged it. In the end, in 1122, after his enemies in Germany had exploited the long dispute – already thirty years old when Henry succeeded to the throne – to weaken royal influence in the German bishoprics and abbeys, Henry agreed to a compromise like that enjoyed by his father-in-law for the past fifteen years.

Chapter Four

Popes and Bishops

What is the meaning of the phrase 'the papal monarchy'? In *41* the eleventh century the structure of government began to develop which gave the papacy and the hierarchy of the Church, between the thirteenth century and the Reformation, a coercive power unique in the history of Christendom. This coercive power presupposed a machinery of government and groups of people in need of coercion. Throughout the early Middle Ages the Church had been strongly authoritarian. At various times the exigencies of a missionary Church had compelled the toleration of paganism; but this was dropped as soon as conveniently possible, and the same tolerance was rarely extended to Christian heretics. Bishops and secular rulers worked closely together for the control of men's souls as well as their bodies. Muslim traders were accepted, Jewish inhabitants of Christendom tolerated and even protected; but apostasy was condemned, and when heresy first began seriously to reappear in the eleventh century, lay rulers and lay mobs took the initiative in consigning the heretics to the flames, the traditional punishment for witchcraft. In the late eleventh century the papal reformers seem to have canalized into orthodox channels the hidden popular religious zeal which had led to the spread of heresy; but this alliance of the hierarchy and popular movements did not last, and in the course of the twelfth century heresy of various kinds became widespread and deeply rooted. It took two main forms: that of the Petrobrusians and Waldensians, essentially an anticipation of Protestant and Puritan doctrines, and that of the Cathars or Albigensians, a dualist or Gnostic group of heresies, fed by missionaries from the East. The dualists preached that the material world was evil, the creation of a wicked angel or god of evil; that goodness could only exist in spirit. They had many adherents in western Germany, the Low Countries and northern France, but it was in southern France and northern Italy that their main strength was concentrated; and in these lands they formed a hierarchy of their own, which was for a time an open and powerful rival to the hierarchy of the Catholic Church. It was these circumstances which led an authoritarian Church to become coercive, and induced among the leaders of the Catholic Church the siege mentality which lasted from the days of Innocent III to those of Pius XII. Innocent's nephew and ultimate successor, Hugolino, Pope Gregory IX (1227–41), curiously combined the roles of patron of St Francis and St Dominic and founder of the Holy Inquisition.

Innocent and Gregory were autocrats, but not despots. Their claims to authority were in principle unlimited; but they knew that in practice they needed earthly allies, colleagues and associates. Especially crucial to both of them were their relations with their cardinals and bishops and with the kings of Germany, by tradition also Holy Roman Emperors. The traditional authority of bishops was strong; and even if this had not been respected by such sticklers for legal respectability as Innocent and Gregory, it was quite impracticable to govern the Church without their co-operation. In a world without modern means of transport and communication, all government had in some sense to be local government, and kings and popes could only govern effectively if they could count on the co-operation of their local officers and colleagues. On this the popes could never entirely count, and papal monarchy in the Middle Ages never in practice attained the authority which it claimed. Theory and practice were always far apart. The authority of popes and bishops was based on similar premises; and although the bishops always had their own local loyalties, and often links with local secular potentates more potent than their loyalty to Rome, bishops and popes were united by their orders, by their education, by their Latin speech, the universal language of the medieval Church, and by some measure of acceptance of the Church's law. At the end of the Middle Ages, especially in the fourteenth and fifteenth centuries, the most remarkable exercise of power in which the popes engaged was the attempt to appoint to bishoprics and benefices, under certain conditions, all over western Christendom, the practice of 'papal provision'. In the twelfth and thirteenth centuries in particular – and in some measure throughout the later Middle Ages – the most stable external manifestation of papal authority was the papal Curia's standing as the supreme appeal tribunal in spiritual cases in Christendom; to it a river of appeals flowed, on cases both serious and absurd.

They came from the courts of archdeacons and bishops, and the effective exercise of papal authority depended on the pope's relations with bishops and other members of the higher clergy. When the tangled matrimonial affairs of an Essex squire came before the pope, or rival claims to a vicarage, or an interminable argument between two schoolmasters, who loved litigation, as to which of them had the right to teach grammar in Winchester, it was scarcely possible for him to elucidate the evidence at a distance of six weeks' or two months' journey from the scene of the dispute. So he laid down the law on the issue involved and left the question of fact to be decided by papal judges-delegate – bishops, abbots, archdeacons; even, in time, rural deans, the N.C.O.s of the medieval hierarchy.

Thus the peasantry of Essex might witness a case of marriage and inheritance being argued in their midst in two courts, royal and papal, according to two sets of law; and it was very frequently a nice problem of argument or diplomacy how the relations between these systems of law and rival courts should be adjudicated. This was only one aspect of the complex relations between clergy and lay folk. In some respects the division between clergyman and layman was one of the

44 Chaucer's parson, from the famous Ellesmere manuscript of the *Canterbury Tales*

most fundamental of social barriers: clerical education, the vow of celibacy and holy orders set the clergy apart. As time went on, more and more laymen acquired some degree of education; it is doubtful if celibacy was ever very effective among the rank and file of the parish clergy in the Middle Ages. And at all times the clergy had ties of every kind with the lay society in which they mingled. Thus Chaucer's

44 parson had a ploughman for brother, and two bishops of Winchester, Henry of Blois (1129–71) and Henry Beaufort (1404–47), were brothers of kings. Thomas Becket, as royal chancellor, had hunted and jousted with king and barons; as archbishop he justified resistance to royal demands by sophisticated clerical arguments. The loyalty of many of King Henry II's barons and knights had something in it of the feeling which had inspired the warriors in the poem on the battle of Maldon (991) to fight and die with their leader.

45 Henry of Blois, Bishop of Winchester, *Henricus episcopus*, in enamels on a gilt copper plaque of a reliquary made for him, now in the British Museum

Words spoken in haste by the king in a violent passion could stir this feeling and lead to murder in Canterbury Cathedral. The feeling was natural and instinctive; yet Christendom was not only shocked by a public act of murder and sacrilege; it was also very much surprised by this treatment of the king's former friend.

Bishop-princes

The paradoxes of a bishop's position come out strikingly in Henry of Blois, the prince-bishop of Winchester. The son of 45 the Count of Blois, and grandson (through his mother) of William the Conqueror, he early joined the great French Abbey of Cluny in which he combined training in the monastic routine and preparation, among other young men of noble birth, for a distinguished career in the Church. He never quite ceased to be either monk or prince. From 1129 he held in plurality the offices of Abbot of Glastonbury, 48 England's oldest and one of its richest abbeys, and Bishop of Winchester, a see which gave its medieval bishops the in- 46, 47 come of multi-millionaires. He thus became a great land-owner and financier; he loved to see a good field of waving corn, and he had a genius for finance. He was a splendid patron, and the list of great treasures he gave or redeemed from pawn for Winchester Cathedral shows that he had an eye akin to Suger's. When his favourite schemes collapsed in the Roman Curia, he consoled himself by buying antique statues and transporting them to Winchester. His affection for Cluny never died, and whenever he found England too hot for him, he retreated to Cluny, characteristically combining enjoyment of the monastic routine that it offered with energetic measures to restore the abbey's finances. He was a great builder, and his cathedral has still some evidences of this; but his most striking monuments are his castles – Wolvesey, Merdon, Farnham, Bishop's Waltham – as much of them as has survived King Henry II's slighting and the ravages of time.

46–48 The prince-bishop. The splendour of Henry of Blois was sustained by the revenues of the bishopric of Winchester, whose Cathedral Treasury (*left*) preserves a memory of Cluniac influence, and those of the abbey of Glastonbury, (*below*). He combined the two offices of bishop and abbot from 1129 until his death in 1171. He never forgot he was a monk by profession, but he prepared for the reign of his brother, King Stephen, by converting Wolvesey Palace within the city walls at Winchester, already a notable stone hall built or rebuilt by his predecessor, into a great castle (*above*)

Henry of Blois was younger brother of King Stephen (1135–54). Under Stephen's rule the country subsided into civil war. In these circumstances the Bishop of Winchester might have been expected to act as mediator between his brother and his cousin Matilda; or he might have been expected to be Stephen's closest supporter. At various times he tried both lines, and thereby discredited himself as a bishop and a statesman. In Stephen's early years Henry was the most forceful and brilliant figure among the English bishops, but for some reason now obscure Stephen would not let him be Archbishop of Canterbury; and although he ruled the English Church for a time as papal 'legate' or representative in England, he suffered for a number of years from thwarted ambition. This combined with a genuine sense of what was due to the Church to make him resist Stephen to the face when he gave some of Henry's fellow bishops cavalier treatment. Henry then tried to sit in judgment on Stephen and Matilda, and even supported Matilda for a time. Thus he became directly involved in the civil war, in siege and counter-siege in his own episcopal city; and it was not soon forgotten that flaming bolts fired from the battlements of Wolvesey started a fire which wasted much of Winchester. To us it seems obvious that Henry had gone too far. Yet for two reasons it was more difficult for Henry to understand this before the outcome made it only too clear to him. First of all, a bishop was an official both of Church and kingdom: he could not stand aloof. Attempts were being made – never wholly successfully – to distinguish more clearly between a bishop's spiritual and secular functions. This might have affected even the Conqueror's grandson, but for the circumstance that a conscientious bishop was also liable to regard himself as acting, like the prophets of the Old Testament, with divine authority, interpreting and enforcing divine sanctions.

Henry's authority as bishop was based on Old Testament precedents, and was also intimately linked with the saints

49 The Emperor Henry VI, 1190–97, one of the most powerful of medieval emperors, whose attempt to unite Germany and southern Italy and Sicily was frustrated for a time by his early death in 1197. From the famous Minnesinger Codex of the early fourteenth century

whose reliquaries he enriched and refurbished in his cathedral, notably that of his obscure but celebrated predecessor, St Swithun. In the same period a humble community in Cornwall was providing a yet more obscure saint with a new shrine. In two ways the reliquary of St Petroc is more remarkable than the far grander one of St Swithun: it still survives, and can be seen in the parish church of Bodmin, Petroc's home; and we can see from its character that it was made and adorned by Arab craftsmen in Norman Sicily. It is one of a number of striking tributes to the close links between the two most highly organized kingdoms of twelfth-century Europe – the kingdom which the Normans had developed on the solid foundations of the Old English monarchy, and that other kingdom, in south Italy and Sicily, which the Normans forged in the same period from Muslim, Greek and native elements.

The Norman principalities in Italy and Sicily were established at the same time as the papal reform; and in the long run the Norman rulers became valuable allies to the popes in their conflicts with the emperors. In the late twelfth century this alliance was threatened when the Emperor Henry VI *49* married the heiress of the Norman kingdom. Henry died young, leaving a disputed succession both in Germany and in Sicily. The immediate threat of encirclement was lifted from the papacy; but when, in the next year (1198), Innocent III mounted the papal throne, he was determined to play an effective and dignified part in settling these difficulties, and especially those in Germany. To state a complex case briefly, Innocent claimed that because the Pope crowned the Emperor, he had the right to sit in judgment on the person of the emperor-elect; and any king of Germany was an emperor-elect. For two years he waited, hoping that the disputants would submit to judgment. When they failed to do so, he proceeded to make his decision. In a secret consistory he argued the case of the two disputants – to whom he added a third, Henry's young son, hitherto too young to be regarded as a serious candidate; and he laid out the case in terms of what was legally right, of what was morally fitting, of what was politically expedient. The third element showed that Innocent realized that it was useless to declare for a theoretically sound candidate if there was no hope of his winning sufficient support. Yet in this lay the weakness of Innocent's position: once he had made his choice, it should have been final, but a change in circumstances could and did alter 'what was expedient', and Innocent found himself committed, with the best of intentions, to fomenting civil war in Germany and changing sides three times. He had ended by committing on the grand scale the error of Henry of Blois.

Chapter Five

The Selection of Popes and Kings

Innocent III's final choice proved successful; but Frederick II 50
of Hohenstaufen, Henry VI's son, grew up to combine the
kingdoms of Sicily and Germany, and however morally
fitting his success may have been, it was politically dangerous
for the papacy. Nor did Frederick show any gratitude to his
maker. Thus it came to pass that in 1241, Pope Gregory IX,
as he lay dying, was fiercely resolved to ensure that his successor should carry on the struggle which had been developing throughout his pontificate between Pope and Emperor.
The Pope might be an autocrat; he might even override (as
Gregory had done) some measure of opposition among the
cardinals to his policies. But when he died it was the cardinals,
not he, who chose his successor, and until that successor was
chosen they acted corporately as the rulers of the Church.
There are now over a hundred cardinals. In the Middle Ages
there could be as many as fifty-three; but in practice the
number often fell below that figure, and in 1241 there were
only thirteen. They were much divided, and Gregory feared
that they would fail to elect a successor to carry on his war
against the Emperor with sufficient dispatch, and perhaps
even fail to elect a successor at all. So he summoned the
Senator of Rome, Matteo Orsini, and gave him certain in-
structions. When the Pope died, the Senator gathered all the
cardinals within reach and hustled them into a Roman palace
which he had fitted out as a prison; there they remained his
prisoners until they had elected a pope. After weeks of
suffering, the cardinals found a means of escape. One of their
number had died; a second was on his deathbed. They hastily
elected him Pope, and in the brief interval before he also went

his way, they had escaped. A few remained in Orsini's power, but their summons to their colleagues to return fell on deaf ears.

'We have turned over among us the innumerable sufferings, the continual heat, the stench, the misery of our confinement, the insults, hunger, famine, sickness by which we were assaulted until life was scarce worth living . . .' – and also the death of two colleagues and the shadow of death hanging over them all. 'We have turned over all this; and we can find no canon which could lead you to summon us for the election in that very place' where the senior cardinal was still held prisoner, 'an insult to the church, a spectacle to the world, to men and angels', and so forth.

'Do you think we have forgotten how we were dragged to prison, bound hand and foot, and beaten like thieves?'; and they proceeded to describe in lurid detail the sufferings of one venerable cardinal who, after assault and battery, was 'hustled through the main streets of the city in a carpet'; also their own

50 The Emperor Frederick II, son of Henry VI, though still a baby at his father's death, was eventually the successful heir to his dominions. Here he is shown in an early manuscript of his own treatise on falconry

sufferings owing to the sanitary arrangements in their prison; and those of another cardinal who was shut in a charnel house, where his warders spat on him and sang comic songs at his expense, not to mention poking their cross-bows at him from under the bed. Finally, the *Duchess of Malfi* touch: 'Nor must it be forgotten that the senator tortured us with terrifying threats, and thundered at us instantly to reveal the new pope when we had elected him, and to speed us on our way he dug up the corpse of the late pope and planted it in our midst. . . .'

In the event, after two years' wrangling, they agreed to the election of Cardinal Sinibaldo Fieschi, who took the name of Innocent IV (1243); and Innocent proceeded at once to show what was the difference between a cardinal and a pope by being converted from a moderate to as implacable an enemy of the Emperor as Gregory IX himself.

Cardinals: the 'Senate' of the Holy See

Thus was the papal conclave born; and in spite of its origins 51, 52 the conclave soon became an established part of the electoral law. The cardinals have ever since had supreme power during a vacancy, but have been effectively prevented from exercising it. The growth of their power was a natural accompaniment to the development of the papal monarchy. The office of cardinal was ancient; but only when the papal reform got under way did the cardinals become a body of papal advisers, of men recruited from all over Europe, able to give the pope aid and counsel, to act as his representatives on embassies. Above all, the revived papacy could not avoid the consequences of being an elective monarchy. If it were to remain powerful and independent, the popes had to be elected by a powerful and independent body. And so the cardinals became the papal chapter, the 'Senate' of the Holy See. In 1059 Pope Nicholas II (whose election had been anything but orderly) passed the first election decree, which placed essential power in the hands of the cardinals. But it was still possible

51, 52 Papal election. These two miniatures from the late fourteenth-century manuscript of Villani's chronicle show the crucial stages in the making of a pope. In the first picture, the cardinals in conclave have made their choice and

for the cardinals to elect two different men as popes, and there was no clear criterion by which the candidates could be judged. It was common for two men to claim to be popes between 1059 and 1179; in that year the danger of a dual election was effectively abolished by the introduction, for the first time in any medieval election, of a majority principle: a vote of two-thirds of the cardinals makes a man pope. The fact that this rule could be made, and could be effective, presupposed that the body of cardinals had achieved sufficient coherence and independence to act as a body, independently (in a measure at least) of the pressures of secular potentates. When they came to be called the 'college' of cardinals, and when (in the mid-thirteenth century) they assumed the red

the pope-elect stands in their midst. In the second, the new pope is shown in St Peter's, holding the symbolic keys, and being crowned with the tiara

hat, which has ever since been their mark of distinction, the cardinals finally became established as the permanent papal council and body of electors.

Their very independence, however, involved a new danger: they might wish to be independent of the pope himself. This might lead, as in 1241–3, to their refusal to elect a pope at all; or it might lead to their rebelling against the pope. In the fourteenth century, when the papacy was settled for two generations at Avignon, a comparatively small body of cardinals acquired habits of authority and a princely standard of living which led them to regard the pope as *primus inter pares*. In 1378, after their return to Rome, a body of cardinals as small as that of 1241 elected a curial official, who they believed would continue to accept their direction, as Pope Urban VI. But the worm turned, and Urban proved violent, tactless and dictatorial. Most of the cardinals fled, and on the pretext that they had elected Urban under pressure, declared his election invalid; they proceeded to elect one of their own number as a rival pope, who settled with his cardinals at Avignon. The Great Schism lasted from 1378 to 1415; before it was finished there were three popes, three colleges of cardinals, and a Church in chaos. The schism was resolved by a General Council, which had always been acknowledged as a possible safeguard if papal authority collapsed, but had only met in recent centuries to confirm papal authority at its height. Since the Council of Constance no pope has resigned or been deposed.

The decree of 1059, broadly speaking, placed the election of the pope in the hands of the cardinals. More precisely, it gave the first voice in the election to the cardinal bishops, who were then joined in the election itself by the other cardinal clergy; and the elect was then acclaimed by the whole clergy and people of Rome and the event notified to the Emperor. What is the meaning of this rigmarole? First and foremost, that a modern notion of election, in which a free decision lies with the majority of a specified body of electors, was quite foreign to the ideas of the early Middle Ages. It was customary to say that popes, bishops and kings were 'elected', 'chosen', in Latin *electi*; but the process of choice belonged to that dream-world of common assumptions which everyone understands and no one can explain. It was often said that the people chose their king; this never happened, in any modern sense of these words. It was often said that God chose popes, bishops and kings; however one may view this notion, it throws little light on the techniques by which God's wishes were interpreted by mortal and fallible men. The word very commonly means 'accepted', and refers to a formal process by which a king was acclaimed by his leading followers. But how did they know whom to acclaim?

King-making was a very formal matter, though behind the forms must have lurked all manner of informal discussions and intrigues. A medieval 'election' survives in fossilized form in the opening ceremony in a modern British coronation, when the Archbishop of Canterbury presents the new sovereign to the people for their acceptance and acknowledgment. This goes back at least to the eleventh century, when the English acclaimed William the Conqueror so vociferously that the Norman guards thought it was a riot. Ideally, the people acclaimed whomsoever the leading dignitary presented to them; the leading dignitary presented whoever had been previously designated by the former king; and the old king designated his eldest son or closest suitable relation. In France the Capetian dynasty produced male heirs with astonishing regularity, and it was normal practice to ensure the succession by 'electing', anointing and crowning the heir in his father's lifetime. This did not usually involve the displacement of the old king, unless (like Louis VI's father) he happened to be in his dotage. It simply underlined the desperate care – only too intelligible to those who who have studied kingship in other societies – to avoid a bloody succession and the abolition of the reigning dynasty. In England lip service was paid to the hereditary principle even in 1066; it became strictly accepted in theory in the twelfth century, but hardly in practice till the thirteenth, when in 1216 the boy-king Henry III succeeded even in conditions of civil war. But the old medley of principles and practices survived for many centuries. When Henry IV usurped the throne in 1399, it was given out that Richard II had voluntarily resigned the throne and designated Henry as his successor, that he had proved unsatisfactory as king and had to be removed, that Henry had been elected by the magnates of the realm, and that he was in any case king by hereditary right. Most of this was probably fiction, but it is all the more revealing for that – revealing of what custom asserted ought to happen in such cases, and of the care which had to be exercised by an insecure king in the late fourteenth century to hide the fact that he had won his throne by war and the people's choice.

The English succession was firmly hereditary, though only fully clarified by statute in the eighteenth century. The French rules were already tolerably fixed, and only differed from the English because the long succession of male heirs between the tenth and the early fourteenth centuries enabled the French lawyers to keep the English Edward III off the French throne by inventing the Salic law, which barred from the throne an heir whose title came through a woman. A new situation produced a new twist in the custom of kingship; and the invention of the Salic law is a very good example of the interplay between politics and law in medieval kingmaking – even if, in this case, the ancient law was in fair measure fictitious. To us it seems natural that if the two conflicted, politics would usually win; and we are inclined to underestimate the force of custom and of law in kingmaking. The speech put into the mouth of the Archbishop of Canterbury early in Shakespeare's *Henry V* is an excellent corrective to this. From 1340 till 1801, with a brief interval after the treaty of Brétigny in 1360, the English kings always claimed also to be kings of France; under Elizabeth I and James I this meant little and mattered much, and it is clear from *Henry V* that Shakespeare and his audience were of the same mind.

> *There is no bar,*
> *To make against your highness' claim to France,*
> *But this, which they produce from Pharamond,*
> *In terram Salicam mulieres ne succedant,*
> *'No woman shall succeed in Salic land':*
> *Which Salic land the French unjustly gloze*
> *To be the realm of France, and Pharamond*
> *The founder of this law and female bar.*
> *Yet their own authors faithfully affirm*

That the land Salic is in Germany,
Between the floods of Sala and of Elbe;
Where Charles the Great, having subdu'd the Saxons,
There left behind and settled certain French;
Who, holding in disdain the German women
For some dishonest manners of their life,
Established then this law; to wit, no female
Should be inheritrix in Salic land. . . .
Then doth it well appear the Salic law
Was not devised for the realm of France;
Nor did the French possess the Salic land
Until four hundred one-and-twenty years
After defunction of King Pharamond,
Idly supposed the founder of this law. . . .

And so on, through a treatise on early French history which
is neither good history nor great poetry. While the constitutional sages gloze, a modern audience is dozing; and
today this passage is commonly either omitted or gagged. Its
solemn deployment by Shakespeare is eloquent testimony of
the living interest of the case in his day.

Of the major European monarchies only the German had
become elective. Down to 1077 the normal process of king-
making in Germany was much as in France and England: the
old king designated, the Archbishop of Mainz designated
again, the princes accepted, the people acclaimed, the Archbishop anointed and crowned. What was special to the
German kings (from the tenth century onwards) was their
right to go to Rome to be anointed and crowned emperors.
But in 1077 there was civil war; and Henry IV was also at
loggerheads with the papacy. In spite of a temporary submission to the Pope, Henry was declared deposed by the
rebel princes, who proceeded to elect one of their own
number as his successor. This was not quite a modern election:
the body of electors was not clearly defined, and so there

could be no strict majority principle; and this piece of king-making was hardly a success. After a few years Henry IV was left in possession of the field. But its memory survived, and when male heirs failed, or archbishops and princes felt disinclined to listen to the old king's voice, something like an election could take place. The growing power of the German dynastic princes, the occasional failure of heirs and conflict with the papacy produced a situation in the late thirteenth century in which the king-emperor was in practice elected by the princes. Inheritance played its part; but the emperors had to accept the consequences of being the creations of the electors, and of owing them some consideration. The process was canonized by Charles IV in 1356, when by the Golden Bull he laid down who the electors were and their rights before the Crown. For the first time a strict electoral principle entered the politics of a secular kingdom. Elsewhere it was held at bay much longer. In the sense that Charles IV's successors were elected, no English king has ever been elected; and the majority principle did not even apply in practice to Members of Parliament – though it crept into the Statute Book in theory in the early fifteenth century – until the nineteenth century.

The Politics of Marriage

Hereditary succession was thus a principle firmly entrenched in most European kingdoms in the later Middle Ages. To choose a king who must rule as well as reign by an accident of birth is a curious proceeding; but the human affection of those in power combined with the urgent need to avoid doubt and disputation to give it a remarkable strength; and custom has never hesitated to consecrate absurdities. It was the inevitable ambition of kings and barons to consolidate and enlarge their domains by successful warfare and judicious marriages; and so marriage in high society became a kind of dynastic game. But just as primogeniture had its compensating advantages, so the subordination of marriage to estate management brought at least one blessing in its wake. The Church had preached monogamy for centuries; but William the Conqueror's great-grandfather had had two wives and his father had none. He was himself the first of his line to be conspicuously faithful to a single wife; piety, affection and the memory of his own fearful childhood played their part in this, but he must also have known that the children he begot were heirs to great and vital possessions. On the whole it seems likely that it was the last of these factors which made (for example) English lay society as strict as the Church on monogamy and stricter than the Church in enforcing the principle that only a legitimate heir could inherit. No doubt the play of human affection, human need and common sense frequently overcame the obstacles to domestic felicity imposed by custom and ambition, but the history of medieval marriage has many ludicrous passages. One of the sensational results of the marriage market was the empire of Henry II *53* who was King of England and Duke of Normandy by inheritance from his mother's father, Count of Anjou by inheritance from his father, and Duke of Aquitaine by his wife's right. This helped to strengthen the marital attitudes of his courtiers. In 1157 Henry fought an unsuccessful campaign in Wales. His Constable was later accused by a fellow-baron of cowardice, fought a duel to prove his innocence, and lost. The result was forfeiture and disgrace; and the Earl of Oxford, who had recently married the Constable's daughter, immediately felt compelled to repudiate his disastrous marriage. When it had been arranged the girl was too young to marry, so she was delivered to the Earl's brother for safe-keeping. The Earl alleged that his brother and fiancée had cohabited; if true, this established a barrier of affinity between them which would be a bar to marriage – a similar allegation was used by King Richard I twenty-five years later to excuse him from marrying the French king's daughter. The girl was locked up and subjected to contumely, but she managed to get her case heard in the Church

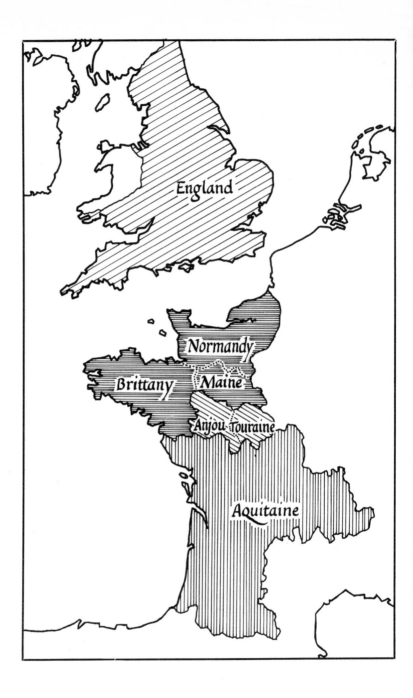

53 The Angevin Empire. The four hatchings show the stages in its growth. Normandy already claimed suzerainty over Maine and Brittany in the eleventh century, and the right to Brittany was secured by the marriage of its heiress to Henry II's son Geoffrey. Henry II was king of England by descent from William I and two Queens Matilda, descendants of the old English line, wives to William I and Henry I; count of Anjou by right of his father; and duke of Aquitaine through his own marriage to Eleanor. Note that English claims in Wales and Ireland and the frontiers of Aquitaine were much more fluid than a single map can show

54 Margaret Beaufort, from a contemporary portrait

courts, which handled matrimonial causes. For political reasons, however, her case proceeded slowly; nearly nine years elapsed before the pope finally insisted that the Earl restore to her the rights of a wife. The Earl complied, and they reared a family together. Of the inwardness of their married life we know nothing; but this preposterous story was the prelude to an outwardly successful marriage.

Nearly three centuries later a girl of twelve, as the result of a vision, accepted a man almost three times her age as her second husband; a few months later he died leaving her pregnant. She married twice more, yet had no more children. It was a strange chance that she had any, stranger still that a single child should have survived the illnesses of childhood and the dangers of a great inheritance. The young Margaret 54 Beaufort had been an eligible widow because the blood of kings flowed in her veins; and her son was the future King 55 Henry VII.

55 King Henry VII, from his effigy by Torrigiani

Chapter Six

Peasants, Townsmen and Landlords

In most parts of medieval Europe, the possession of land was the basis of livelihood, wealth, social status and government. The peasant lived by what he tilled; the warrior-aristocrat fed *56–58* on the produce of his land, owed his income to its surplus or *61* its rents, his standing to the breadth of his acres and the numbers of his tenantry and followers. A feudal society was a society in which social bonds and legal status were inextricably entangled with land tenure. Yet every country had its cities, and in some parts of Europe town predominated over village as a social centre, a centre of government, of population and of wealth. Peasant, landlord and burgher might lead very different lives; but they were closely interwoven; and each has left substantial traces of his presence on the face of western Europe as we see it today – though at first sight not all the groups in proportion to their numbers. Let us try to discern something of how each of them has left its trace, and and how each was related to the other.

The Peasants

In the Middle Ages the vast majority of the population of western Europe were peasants, living off what they grew, tilling their own small plots or working for their neighbours and their lords; in either event, living close to the soil, in cottage or hovel, with a standard of living which would today be regarded as harsh and precarious. Life was hard; the prospect of real prosperity slight. This was true everywhere and all the time. Yet there was change too, and a measure of change which made little difference to the life of the many, yet

56, 57 Peasant life. *Left:* the parable of the Labourers in the Vineyard, from an eleventh-century manuscript. At the top, the master of the vineyard hires labourers in the market-place at different hours; in the middle they till the vineyard; below they are given their reward, and on the right the explanation. *Above:* the grape-harvest, from an English misericord (tip-up seat) of the fourteenth century in Gloucester Cathedral. The Gloucester misericords include several scenes from country life; no doubt this was intended to portray the season of autumn

58 *Right:* harrowing and sowing the winter corn, from a scene representing October, *Octobris,* in a calendar of the early sixteenth century

a fundamental difference to a few, and laid foundations from which greater social and economic changes were to grow in much more recent times.

59   Let us contemplate two pictures. First, a corrugated pasture in a Buckingham landscape. The corrugations still reveal the pattern of the strips of an open field before the enclosure movement of the eighteenth and early nineteenth centuries.

59   *Below:* Padbury, Buckinghamshire, showing corrugated pasture representing medieval strips. In this aerial photograph the strips carry straight through the later hedges of the enclosure movement. A sixteenth-century map proves that we are looking at medieval strips

60 *Above:* country life in France, outside the walls of Paris, showing the Ile de la Cité, Sainte-Chapelle and the royal palace. From the *Très Riches Heures du duc de Berry*

Their lines continue across the encloser's hedges, their number and shape conform to those laid out in a sixteenth-century map. We are looking at a medieval open field. In fields such as this, lords' and peasants' strips were scattered, according to a pattern sometimes rational, sometimes (by the end of the Middle Ages) higgledy-piggledy. The shape of the strip was dictated by the use of a heavy plough in the English claylands. Anyone who has ever fought with clay in a garden knows how heavy it is to turn, how difficult to drain; but if this is achieved, there comes a correspondingly high reward. A heavy plough pulled by several oxen (in later times by horses, too) solved the first problem; the scheme of ploughing left a furrow or gulley every few yards into which the water might drain, and so the second be solved. But a heavy plough with a team of oxen was an expensive piece of equipment, beyond the resources of a single peasant; and scattered strips could not be tilled by private enterprise. Common understandings

56–58 for ploughing, sowing, reaping – and above all for weeding
60 and for ensuring that a lazy farmer's weeds did not spoil his more energetic neighbours' strips – were clearly essential; and the strips were themselves part of much larger fields, on which single crops in two years would be followed by an idle year of fallow, by a simple rotation.

In determining the small arrangements and the large a great measure of common action by the village community was needed; in accord, doubtless, with the lord and his steward and bailiff. The lord's involvement depended in a measure on the extent to which he drew his income from rent, or the extent to which he drew it by direct farming, to raise corn or wool to feed and clothe his household and for sale in the market. In the latter case, especially when his strips were scattered among his tenants', he was as much involved in the common enterprise (in the person of his servants) as the peasants; it was a communal effort in which lord and peasants joined; and in a society with a seasonal rhythm, whose life and prosperity depends on the harvest, there must always be

61 Peasants at work, actually the Israelites in Egypt, from an eleventh-century English manuscript, Ælfric's paraphrase of the *Pentateuch* and *Joshua*

a degree of common interest and purpose less apparent in more developed and specialized economies. Conflict there was; but it is wrong to assume that the battles which are recorded – local strife against a lord's bailiff, or against a lord's insistence that all corn be ground in his mill and be subject to the payment of his miller's fees – were the core of the relation of peasant and lord. The underlying sense of community was a vital element in the open-field village.

Our second picture is of vineyards on terraces in the Apennines. No one can say precisely how old these terraces *62* are, or how long they have carried vines. But they represent, at one time and another over two or three millennia, a measure of common effort and foresight by lord and peasant cultivators alike. The terraces themselves represent a large investment of human effort; the vines take five years, and the olives that flourish on many similar terraces a decade, to mature sufficiently to reward their cultivators. As with the rubber plantations in the twentieth century, the prospect of a rich reward here inspired peasants as well as lords to invest their effort for what must have seemed at times a distant future.

In the early Middle Ages, between the fifth and the ninth centuries, in both northern and southern Europe, the life of the peasant was very close to the subsistence level. By the twelfth and thirteenth centuries the use of money, the growth of trade and the organization of charity by the Church had all conspired to create reserves against the disaster inevitable in earlier times if the harvest was bad. But the harvest still mattered very deeply; natural disaster, drought, flood, plague or cattle murrain, still affected rich and poor alike; and the memory of a subsistence society was not lost. In such a world it is assumed that the community is governed by mutual aid; that the reserves of all are at the disposal of the unfortunate. Life may be harsh, but it is mitigated by the sense of community.

The corrugated fields of Padbury and the delectable terraces of the Cinqueterre remind us of the areas of life in which lord and peasant shared a common interest; of the common pattern of life over the centuries and over wide areas of Europe. The deserted villages of late medieval England, which numbered many hundreds, remind us of change and conflict.

The Bubonic Plague, which set in all over Europe in 1347–8, and recurred at intervals from the fourteenth to the seventeenth centuries, was the most notorious solvent of social and economic change. The sudden removal, in England,

62   Terraces in the Apennines. Vineyards in the Cinqueterre, near Genoa

of perhaps a third of a community by the ravages of a horrible disease was traumatic in itself; it involved also social dislocation in a slow-moving, traditional society, of a kind unprecedented in human memory; and this in its turn bred an uncertainty, a malaise, a suspicion which brought conflict and change. The English landlord found that his labourers' wages had inordinately increased. We can see that this was due to a sudden dearth of labour, a natural price increase to meet an unprecedented scarcity. The landlord, knowing nothing of nineteenth- and twentieth-century economics, attributed the demand to human wickedness, and pressed for laws to check this sudden overflowing of peasant depravity. Thus misunderstanding and conflict grew; and a chain of events led to the Peasants' Revolt. For many peasants, higher wages and more land free to buy and cultivate had meant prosperity; they looked for more and found their hopes frustrated by the resistance of the landlords, which to them seemed blind rapacity. Thus the traditional pattern of life was dislocated.

The fall in population, new opportunities, and the disappearance of old, led to a sharp fall in the population of many villages. By the mid-fifteenth century a number had almost disappeared. Little corn was grown in them; the landlord looked askance at the small rents they brought him. His steward and accountants told him that the price of wool was rising, the price of corn falling; the lawyers assured him that the remaining tenants could easily be evicted, bought out or transferred to neighbouring towns. And so, in Thomas More's famous phrase, 'the sheep, which were wont to be so meek and tame and so small eaters now, as I hear say, be become so great devourers and so wild that they eat up and swallow down the very men themselves. They consume, destroy and devour whole fields, houses and cities.'

63   The traces of lost villages, which have been detected in so many parts of England, tell stories such as this. Each has its own tale, often now beyond recovery; and our brief sum-

63 The traces of a lost village, Burston, Buckinghamshire, as revealed in an aerial photograph by Dr St Joseph. The village centre, with rectangular *messuages* (houses and gardens) between streets, some straight, some meandering, is very clearly marked in this photograph

mary does no justice to a complex and intriguing pattern of change which transformed the English countryside. Quite a different story lies behind the peaceful upland pastures of *64, 65* Schwyz and Uri and their wooded neighbours, the small central cantons in which Switzerland was born. To the traveller they represent an eternal, changeless, traditional way of life; and it is true that there is much in common between their life today and in the thirteenth century. Yet on these peaceful pastures there arose, unaffected by books or schools or substantial outside influences, peasant communities which had no local lords at all, and came to dedicate their spare energies to checking, defeating and destroying more distant overlords. The story of William Tell and the Habsburg bailiff Gessler is perhaps pure legend; but it correctly symbolizes the destruction of hierarchy in a part of Europe where the normal structure of medieval society seemed even then wholly irrelevant. From the peaceful pastures of Schwyz came the first of the Switzer pikemen, who formed the nucleus of the most dreaded fighting force in late medieval Europe and gave their name to Switzerland, most bellicose of countries in the fifteenth century, however it may be to us a symbol now of peace as well as of freedom.

64, 65   Upland pastures in Schwyz and Uri. Meadows round St Meinrad, an ancient church in Baroque disguise. This grassland was used for summer pasture already in the early Middle Ages. Similarly, the men of Uri must have used the Klausenpass in the Middle Ages, since it linked a small corner of the Canton to its main territory; the photograph *opposite* shows pasture and forest just below the pass

In eastern Europe, especially in Poland, corn flourished and was exported in the late Middle Ages; landlords grew stronger, peasant freedom declined, and the shackles of serfdom grew, to mark a whole society until the nineteenth century, when humanitarianism and the collapse of the corn market due to American competition led to the freeing of the serfs. In the west this liberation came in the centuries following the Black Death. Prudent, hard-working peasants had always added field to field; now their opportunities were multiplied. Rich peasants prospered; their sons entered the gentry. Chaucer's Frankeleyn was in origin a free peasant – that is what the word means – but he had grown rich, become a yeoman farmer, then (in wealth at least) a member of the gentry, and an MP. In all the complexities of change in the late Middle Ages there were many such. Yet the poor remained poor; the large majority of the peasantry were little removed from their former way of life; and Tudor legislation reveals that the breakdown of medieval patterns of social relief, of medieval charity, of the medieval Church, left in a country in which many were growing richer a problem of poverty of new and frightening dimensions.

Towns and Townsfolk

Two kinds of memorial surviving from the Middle Ages bring to life, most vividly and most concretely, the society of the past: the remains of monasteries and the remains of cities. Town life was no novelty in the Europe of the eleventh and twelfth centuries; it had been the basis of Roman civilization, 66 and for all that the decay of Roman cities was the chief outward sign of its departure, many towns survived, especially in southern Europe. Yet even in Italy they were reduced to shadows, and the city-state which was to be as characteristic of Italy in the trecento and the quattrocento as of Greece in the fifth and fourth centuries B C was essentially a new growth on an ancient root. In precisely the same period towns grew and flourished all over northern Europe; many on old foundations, as in Italy, but only a few after continuous occupation from Roman times. Thus in the south the growing towns reflected a traditional way of life revived and extended; in the north a pattern of living essentially new.

With these differences went two others, a political and a social, both equally necessary to an understanding of the place of the towns in medieval society. In the long run the Italian cities threw off the yokes of kings and princes, of local feudal nobles and the distant emperor alike; they formed republics and achieved a degree of independence in mind and fact which is one of the striking points of similarity to the ancient cities of Greece. Like the Greek cities, the republics saw many vicissitudes: internal strife and warfare between

66 Continuity in city life. This massive Etruscan gate at Perugia, with an arch rebuilt in Roman times and surmounted by a Renaissance loggia, links three of the ages of the city's prosperity

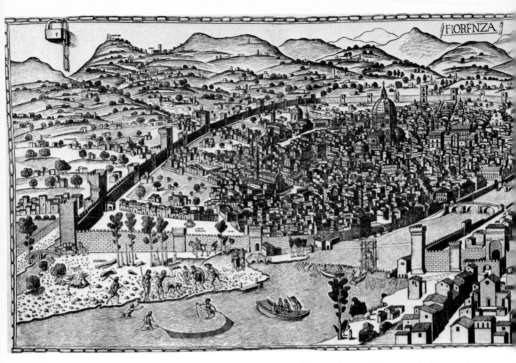

cities were endemic, and in the end empires and despotisms
arose, and freedom became a treasured memory; but not
before it had carved its image deep in the European con-
sciousness. By a curious irony, it is not among the great city-
states of Italy in which the civilization of the Renaissance grew
and flourished that any continuous tradition of freedom or
democracy was born, but among the obscure, remote peasant
communities which emerged in the thirteenth century as the
first confederate cantons of Switzerland. Confederate by
necessity, independent by instinct and genius, the Swiss cantons represent in miniature the many forces opposed to
authority and subjection and the normal hierarchy of medieval society.

In the twelfth and thirteenth centuries these forces could
be seen at work in countless medieval cities great and small,
in the movement to form communes, communities of
citizens sworn to uphold their common interest against
higher powers and enemies of every kind. But it is a mistake

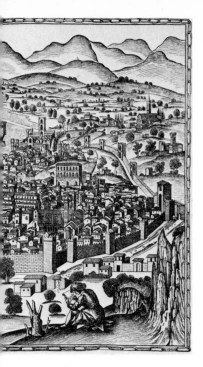

67 Italian cities. Florence in the late fifteenth century, showing many familiar buildings, and how the enceinte of the walls built in the fourteenth century still left plenty of open space within

to see the origin and flowering of medieval towns in terms of a dialectic between burgess and king, prince or feudal noble. In England the first renaissance of town life came in the late ninth and tenth centuries, directly and self-consciously fostered by King Alfred and his son. Again, in the twelfth and thirteenth centuries, over a hundred new towns were founded by the English kings and the English nobility; many more were built in Gascony under the patronage of the same *72* dynasty. Nor was this (as was once supposed) a phenomenon of northern Europe. In most Italian communes in early days feudal nobles and their sons played a leading part; conflicts there were, but they arose out of the bonds of common interest which alone made the renaissance of town life possible in every part of Europe.

The social difference between north and south was that in great measure the Italians became once again town dwellers – peasants, artisans, merchants, knights and noblemen jostled each other in the streets of Italian cities, as in *Romeo and Juliet*.

68–70 Three towns, successive capitals of the Viricones or Wrekin folk. *Above:* the Wrekin, where the ditches of the prehistoric hill-fort and town can still be traced. *Top right:* Roman Viriconium, on the plain at its feet. *Bottom right:* Saxon and Norman Shrewsbury, built in a bend of the Severn not far away

Most northern towns had peasants too, at least in early days; and most towns were by modern standards on the scale of large villages. Twenty thousand made a great city, fifty thousand a giant. There were exceptional areas in the north, like parts of Flanders, where the population of the towns exceeded that of the countryside. But the northern lord and peasant were country dwellers; their lands predominantly agricultural; their towns, for the most part, market towns, vital to the life of the country round them, but not dominating it as did the Italian.

When King Alfred built his *burhs*, his boroughs or fortress towns, they were in the first instance centres for refuge and defence against the Danes. Such centres for refuge and defence had been built on many English hill-tops before the Romans came, as Old Sarum and Maiden Castle and the Wrekin and a score of others bear witness. A few had even become permanent settlements. But what is striking about

68–70

71 Trier. This eighteenth-century engraving still shows how the medieval city only occupied about half of the large Roman enceinte: the bridge on the right of the picture was actually in the middle of the Roman city, which stretched far away to the right

72 Armagnac. A characteristic bastide, or small fortress market-town, of which hundreds were built in the south of France in the twelfth and thirteenth centuries. The grid of streets centres on the market, and is surrounded by walls

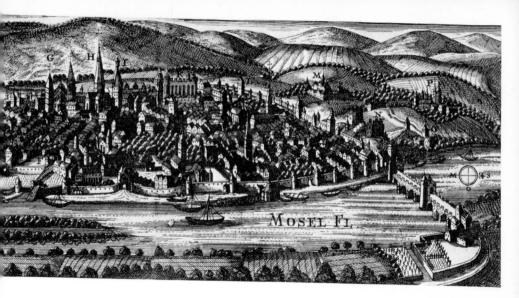

MOSEL FL.

Alfred's towns is that from the moment that his imaginative brain conceived them, they were more than fortresses – centres of life, of civilized activity as well as strongholds. The social pattern of medieval towns was always complex, from their foundation, though much more complex in later centuries than at first.

The mingling of function of medieval towns is well illustrated by their most conspicuous visible feature. The walls and towers and gates made them defensible; formidable defensive works, often placed in Italy on hill-tops or steep slopes difficult to scale. Defence was always liable to be one step ahead of attack in medieval warfare, and the power of more than one great medieval emperor foundered when faced by a coalition of walled cities whose gates were barred to him. Yet often the walls and gates survived and were kept *71* in repair long after the rise of artillery at the end of the Middle Ages, sometimes long after the likelihood of a siege had become exceedingly remote. This reflects their other function as customs barriers, marking the limit of the city's valuable privileges, balking smugglers, ensuring that all goods which came to the market or the shops of the city had passed through the gates and paid their tolls.

73 Alnmouth, a new town of the twelfth century, built by the Vescy lords of Alnwick as an outlet for their produce and a supply base for their household

74 Durham, an old town, designed by nature as a fortress not far from the Scots frontier and fortified anew by bishops and monks in the eleventh and twelfth centuries against enemies spiritual and temporal. Cathedral, monastic precinct and castle occupy so much of the main site that from quite early days the little town spilt across the bridge to the right (south)

To these two functions corresponded the most permanent elements in town society, soldiers and merchants. Towns there were, without walls and without soldiers, but not many; and the more independent the towns, the more they needed soldiers. No sensible definition of a medieval town can exclude a market; and it could scarcely exist in any useful sense without merchants. In early days even knights and merchants were not wholly distinct; as time went on an ever greater diversity appeared, so that the society of a late medieval town was diverse and specialized.

75

The vast majority of towns were market towns, natural centres of an agricultural district. They grew in response to many impulses, but above all to provide a proper setting for the minting and effective use of money. For several centuries in the early Middle Ages western Europe had had no silver currency – a little gold, useful for buying costly silks from the Orient or a platoon of slaves, or as ornaments for rich men's wives, useless for small change or the ordinary purchase of sheep, cattle, food and clothing in moderate quantities. From the eighth and ninth centuries on, a silver currency grew up in every land; to be joined once again by a flourishing gold coinage when, in the twelfth and thirteenth centuries, the florin and the ducat began their long reign over the Mediterranean. Money meant that feudal lords could lease or mortgage their domains to supply the sinews of higher living standards, costlier houses, larger households, more grandiose tournaments and wars. The households must be fed and clothed, and this came in due course to provide occupation for weavers, fullers and dyers, who in their turn had to be fed. The products of the land had increasingly to be marketed to provide food and raw materials for artisans, food and clothing for growing battalions of domestic servants, armed retainers and mercenaries – and for the other folk who lived and ate but were not themselves producers: knights, monks, nuns, and most of the clergy. Thus the market became the centre of much that was vital and much that was new in medieval society, the centre of every town.

This was true whatever the origin of the town; equally true was its close links with, its close dependence on the country around, from which a high proportion of its people came. Every town of any substance probably grew faster in the twelfth and thirteenth centuries than the natural growth of its population. The Italian cities showed their status as independent powers by regulating every event in the lives of their citizens and the country district or *contado* surrounding each. We may doubt whether much attention was commonly paid to many such regulations; their urgent repetition sometimes proves that it was not. But they show the city fathers' aspirations, and they show often in a mirror how the people of city and *contado* behaved. Sometimes immigration was forbidden, to ensure that there were peasants to till the lands; often whole villages were emptied to people the city – in the great days of expansion in the thirteenth century, however much tension might arise, however frequent lawsuits, riots, sorties, wars, and rumours of war might be, town and country flowed in and out of each other, and only occasionally, in artificial circumstances, would they be wholly alien. No doubt some of the new towns planted in Wales by Edward I or in central and eastern Europe by German lords were an alien presence among folk of strange speech and foreign manner of life. Some great ports, like the cities of the Hanseatic League, Bergen, Hamburg, Lübeck, Danzig and the rest, were international centres, with a rapidly shifting population, a large proportion without roots in the neighbouring country. Every really great city had such a cosmopolitan element; an English community (a rare phenomenon in the south outside the great centres of learning or the Church, Bologna and Rome) flourished in Genoa. Scandinavian and French communities played a conspicuous part in

76, 77   Spoleto, a hill town provided naturally for defence, but ill-provided with water. The great fortress, or Rocca, at Spoleto, and the huge aqueduct, rebuilt in the Middle Ages on Roman foundations, illustrate this very clearly. The view *above*, from the south-east, also shows the outer wall of the city falling away to the left; in the lower picture the city is viewed, as it were, by a bird flying in from the north – the aqueduct is hidden by the Rocca, top left, and the same city wall runs away to the right and then skirts round the lower city and back up to the Rocca

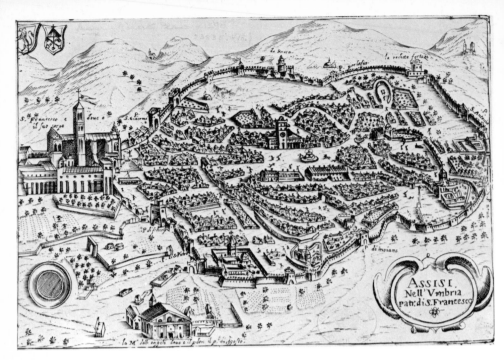

78, 79   Assisi. *Above:* a sixteenth-century engraving. To the left, the Basilica of St Francis stretches out over the plain; top centre, the Rocca marks the summit of the foot-hill on which Assisi stands; to the right begin the slopes of Monte Subasio (see pl. 17). *Opposite:* a characteristic street

eleventh-century London; a German hanse was established there at least from the twelfth century. But in London, as in most cities, the native element still predominated, to the extent that it remained conspicuously an English city even a generation after the Norman Conquest.

In lesser cities the population must always have been mainly of local extraction, though not necessarily for that *76–79* reason of narrow horizon. Spoleto and Assisi doubtless drew their folk from the valley of Spoleto at their feet. A twelfth-century merchant of Assisi might prosper sufficiently to carry his wares as far afield as France. The son might react against the power of the counting house by first dreaming of chivalry and knightly adventure with a troop of mercenaries; and finally throw in his lot with the Lady Poverty, and found

an international order of Friars. The wheel has come full cycle, and Assisi has the mark of its greatest son upon it; to the apostle of poverty it owes the pilgrims and tourists on which it thrives. Yet Francis, though a saint of universal fame, remains a native of Assisi, and the perfect medieval city in which he was born is as essential for the understanding of the saint, as are his shrine and his basilica, set fortress-like in defiance of the neighbouring communes, in defence of the city's most precious possession, the saint's relics, to understanding the nature of a small Italian commune.

Assisi and Spoleto reveal to the most casual visitor both the continuity of their history from Roman times (pre-Roman times indeed), and the inconvenience of living on a hill-top. Both are comparatively rare in northern cities. Great abbeys created and preserved the hill-top towns at St Albans, where St Alban was believed to have been martyred, and Battle, where King Harold undoubtedly fell.

80 More characteristic of the English scene is Old Sarum, a dry and windswept prehistoric fort, restored in late Saxon and early Norman times as a fortress, enclosing a cathedral close, with a group of suburbs growing round it to make the semblance of a town; but soon deserted for the lush meadows of the River Avon where New Sarum stands.

In St Francis's early years a new town was growing up by another River Avon. Stratford grew rapidly into a modest market town, drawing the bulk of its people from the district round about. In this case the names of its early inhabitants, listed in thirteenth-century surveys, reveal with unusual clarity the places round from which the early generations came, and the more distant homes of just a few. Here is the beginning of an ordinary market town, like Assisi, and the community of Stratford-on-Avon was able to produce, and educate, in later times, a man as remarkable as Francis, and become in like manner the centre of a cult.

The *contadini*, in eleventh-, twelfth- and thirteenth-century Italy, came into the cities as peasants and lords. The

torre and the feuds came too, and lend an air of feudal   *81*
absurdity to the sky-line and the social chronicle of many
cities. But in every city – north and south of the Alps –
streets and *quarters* gathered shop-keepers and artisans of
common interest, and groups of other kinds – in Milk Street,
and Bread Street, and in many a butchers' Shambles; in   *82*
Cheaps and Coney and Poultry markets; in Roper Street,
Cordwainer Street, the Drapery, the Mercery – and their
equivalents in German, French, Italian and Spanish; in Old
and New Jewry, in London and other English cities between
the Norman Conquest and the Expulsion (1290), or in the
Saracen and Greek quarters of Norman Palermo.   *83*

80   Old Sarum. The Norman castle motte and cathedral within the prehistoric
ramparts

82　*Above:* the Shambles in York, which still show the shape and structure of a
late medieval street. In London (see p. 105), nothing can now be seen of the
medieval Shambles (literally, the meat market)

81　*Left:* a lofty *torre* in Perugia survives as a reminder of the military, feudal
section of its population, and of how the knights of the *contado* often came to live
in cities such as this in the twelfth and thirteenth centuries

83 *Left*: the quarters of Palermo, from a manuscript of 1195–96. This picture shows a formalized map or panorama of the city, with gardens, palatine chapel, port and castle, and the various peoples who lived in different quarters of the city

84 *Right*: Siena and the Virtues, the city represented as an old man surrounded by Faith, Charity, Hope, Prudence and Magnanimity; the inscription reads C.S.C.C.V. (the second C is an addition): *Communa Senarum Civitatis Virginis* – a detail from *Good Government*, by Ambrogio Lorenzetti (see pl. 85)

The feudal nobles sometimes came to live in the cities; more often they had town houses and expected to wield influence commensurate with their own view of their standing in the world; more often still they sent their younger sons to follow their own fortune or repair the family's in the multifarious activities of the city. Over most of western Europe, kings and princes alternately fostered and checked the growth of towns – the sinews of their wealth and power, but tending to aspire to excessive independence; in either event they looked coolly at Montagues and Capulets. In northern Italy rich merchants, lawyers and land agents (in so far as they were socially distinct from the feudal nobles and their families) insisted on taking the reins of government when external powers and the traditional authority of the local bishop had been overcome. Yet this rarely led to stable government for any length of time; sometimes the noble, the rich and the poor (or moderately poor) disputed one with another; more commonly alliances arose, and factions, which were solved, or partly solved, by bitter fighting or by calling in an umpire, the *podestà*, commonly a member of another city, whose essential function was to act as referee in the sport of civic faction and freedom. Eventually the freedom decayed, and the Sforzas and Visconti vaunted their power, or the Medici subtly manipulated; and so the Renaissance flourished in a world in which a measure of peace had replaced a measure of freedom. But if the free republics had never existed, our civilization would be much the poorer.

Through the centuries from the eleventh to the fifteenth one trend can be discerned in every city of any consequence, northern or southern: the growing definition of citizenship. The lord with a town house; the peasant who happened to live within the walls; the monks or canons of a religious house within the city; the clergy of its parish churches; the cordwainers and haberdashers who had grown up in the city; the well-to-do foreigners from ten or fifty or five hundred miles away: all in early days could equally be accounted citizens. This never meant equality; but as the privileges of citizenship grew, and a measure of community arose among the citizen body, so a tendency to democracy led to a tendency to build walls round the citizenry as well as round their city. Birth, long residence or purchase formed in all manner of different ways the basis of a privilege increasingly defined; and the movement reflects the growing aspiration of the city to lead its own life, independent of, or as lord of, its *contado*, sometimes almost oblivious of the roots from which it sprang; but fostering the sense of civic pride which was to be one of the most conspicuous outward signs of the Renaissance.

84–85

85 Siena and *Good Government*. Another detail from the painting by Ambrogio Lorenzetti, showing the well-governed Sienese enjoying the fruits of peace and good order, attending a sermon and dancing in the piazza

86, 87 Castles. *Left:* Conisborough, an English baronial keep of the late twelfth century. *Right:* Ludlow. The walls, mainly of the eleventh century surmounted by towers mainly of the early fourteenth century, symbolize the formidable image that Norman barons and the first Earl of the March, Roger Mortimer, who died in 1330, wished to present to the Welsh.

The Landlords

A great landlord valued his land for the number of tenants it could hold, whom he could summon to his standard in time of war, and for the silver it brought into his money-chests. In the early Middle Ages, on the whole, he was more interested in providing himself with warriors; as the centuries passed his tastes became more expensive, more varied and more sophisticated; and even for his wars money, which could hire men and buy supplies, might be more useful than tenants. He or his tenants needed to find good markets for the produce of their fields – corn, wool, meat and so forth; markets which would attract merchants from near and far to carry such of their produce as was not consumed nearby to places where it could be used, and also to bring to the local markets metal for his weapons, cloth for his liveries, carpets and tapestries to adorn his castles, silks for his wife, spices for his kitchen and (in southern Europe at least) slaves to serve in his household.

Between the eleventh and the thirteenth centuries the need for money rose sharply. The standard of living and of civilization of the nobility rose; but their chief extravagances continued to be in building and warfare. In the golden age of castle-building these activities were often not distinct; and some of the reasons for the growing need for money can be brought home vividly to us if we compare the simple earth 88 mound, shown in the Bayeux Tapestry, which formed the 89 basis of the motte-and-bailey castle of the eleventh century,

with the more elaborate stone structures of the same age, such as the Tower of London; or again, with the growing elaboration of ring walls, towers and living-quarters of the castles of Henry of Blois or those the Crusaders built in Palestine and Syria; or with the final development of the medieval castle in those of Edward I, with their elaborate rings of walls, and their intricate devices to give the defenders command of every line of fire, and to counter every move of the besiegers. These were royal castles, and the immense sums spent by Edward I in castle-building help to explain the chronic financial difficulties of his later years, which embroiled even so strong and effective a king with his subjects. If the king was in constant financial trouble, one can understand why even the wealthiest of lesser men were concerned to make the most of their resources. Hence their patronage of towns, behind whose walls permanent markets could convert their produce into silver, and their silver into the needs and luxuries of the age.

47, 90

88 The Norman motte or mound being built. The Normans preparing to defend themselves before the Battle of Hastings. From the Bayeux Tapestry

89–91 Three castles. *Above:* Berkhamsted, the perfect outline of a Norman motte-and-bailey castle in England. Originally the motte had a wooden tower on its summit, the earth ramparts a stockade of some kind, later replaced by stone keep and wall. *Right:* Kerak, a great crusading castle of the twelfth century, with a large keep surrounded by curtain walls more elaborate than the first enceinte at Ludlow (88). *Below:* Angers, a major castle rebuilt in the thirteenth century, with round towers to give the archer within widest opportunity and no corner for the sappers to mine

92–93 The Crusades, temporal and spiritual. *Right:* Jerusalem, centre of the crusading movement, represented the goal of the warfare of the spirit and the Holy War on earth. But the whole Muslim and infidel world was a possible field for crusading zeal: St Louis died at Tunis in 1270. *Above:* he sets out from Paris, blessed by a procession of monks

Ways to Salvation: Pilgrims and Crusades

Building and war were combined in the most powerful of medieval weapons, the castle. Extravagant building, however, was not only indulged in to provide a lord with domestic and military equipment; it catered also for the salvation of his soul. Immense sums were lavished on the building of monasteries and churches, monuments to the piety or troubled conscience of their patrons, in which the most fervent prayers available could ceaselessly argue their case at the gate of Heaven. For a short period temporal and

92, 93   spiritual ends were joined together in the notion of the Crusade – a short period, that is, if one considers the real vogue and practical effectiveness of the Crusades, which lasted only from 1096 to the early thirteenth century. The fashion, however, did not die quickly; even in the fifteenth century a conscientious pope might still think it one of his primary tasks to launch a Crusade.

94–96 The pilgrimage to St James. One of the most popular of medieval pilgrimages was that to Santiago (St James) de Compostela in north-western Spain. *Right:* St James himself in pilgrim costume, a fifteenth-century statue at Semur-en-Auxois. *Above:* St James as a crusader, slaying the Muslim, from the late twelfth-century tympanum of Compostela Cathedral. *Opposite:* the Cathedral nave, early twelfth century

98 *Above:* the return from Santiago: pilgrims playing games to shorten the journey. From the fifteenth-century *Hours of the Duchess of Burgundy*

97 *Left:* Christ as pilgrim, with staff and cockle, on the road to Emmaus, but dressed as for the road to Santiago. An eleventh-century relief at S. Domingo de Silos, Spain

Next to church-building the most popular traditional technique for medieval laymen actively to pursue the path to heaven was by going on pilgrimage. The spiritual treasury of medieval Europe was inexhaustible. Every church had its relics; most great churches had the shrine of a local saint who attracted pilgrims from his own country. Richest in saints and relics was Rome itself, which in the early Middle Ages had been viewed more as the home of the saints, a centre of pilgrimage, than as a seat of government. Second only to Rome in popularity and efficacy was the pilgrimage to St James, Santiago de Compostela in north-western Spain; and the pilgrim routes through southern France and northern Spain carried the pilgrim past the shrines of numerous saints less eminent than St James the Apostle, but far from negligible.

95, 97
99–103

94, 96

For those who loved adventure, or whose sins were desperate, there was also the pilgrimage to the Holy Land itself.

A barbarian king of an earlier century, in the process of receiving instruction in the Christian faith, was supposed to have said that if he and his warriors had been present at Calvary, things would have turned out differently. As the centuries passed the need to consecrate the warlike activities of a warrior aristocracy was increasingly felt; and at many different levels the idea was current that lance and sword could be used to do God's work. The popes of the late eleventh century developed the idea of a holy war in defence of Christendom, for the 'defence' or recovery of lands which had once been Christian, and especially of Jerusalem and Palestine; a war which God would bless since it served His purposes, and which would lead Him also to give His blessing, and salvation, to those who engaged in it: a noble idea in its way, if one ignores its consequences. More immediately reflected in action was the popular idea which gave it violent and widespread effect: that a special climacteric was at hand when men should arise with God's blessing *105* to slaughter His enemies, be they Jews (never before massacred in western Europe) or Muslims. In fairness, one must remember that the Church's leaders were trying to chisel a very stony problem: how to curb the violence of a society bred to war and to draw out its potential idealism. The popes themselves not only had a reasonable fear of the consequences of Turkish military success, but also an excessive trust in the capacity of earthly weapons to fulfil what they believed to

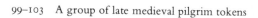
99–103   A group of late medieval pilgrim tokens

104   A round church. After the First Crusade the fashion was revived for a time, especially in England, of building churches with circular naves in imitation of the Church of the Holy Sepulchre in Jerusalem. Holy Sepulchre, Cambridge, probably built for a small community of Canons of the Holy Sepulchre in the early twelfth century, is the earliest surviving example from Norman England

be God's purposes. The First Crusade was remarkably
successful: Jerusalem was captured and remained in Christian
hands for nearly a century; a large throng of the most violent
elements in western society were removed to a safe distance.
It is probable that the Crusades played a large part in helping
to make western Europe a somewhat more peaceable area
than it had been hitherto. They also played a part in the
expansion of Christendom in the twelfth and thirteenth
centuries, as growing population led to a period of coloniza-
tion, within and without the established frontiers of western
Europe. In some measure these factors were known and
appreciated by the Church's leaders; they were aware, too,
that the Crusades brought out the depths of human squalor
as well as notable and devoted heroism. Yet they were
primarily concerned with the defence of Jerusalem and the
conquest or reconquest of lands from Islam.

Chapter Seven

The Beggar and the Pope

There was another way of pursuing these aims. Most of the famous stories about St Francis come from biographers writing after his death and canonization. One of them, however, was narrated by a French bishop in Syria in a letter written a few days, or at most a few weeks, after the event. 'Master Reiner, prior of St Michael, has entered the order of the Brothers Minor, an order which is multiplying rapidly on all sides, because it imitates the primitive Church and follows the life of the Apostles in everything. The master of these brothers is named Brother Francis; he is so lovable that he is venerated by everyone. Having come into our army, he has not been afraid, in his zeal for the faith, to go to that of our enemies. For days together he announced the word of God to the Saracens, but with little success; then the Sultan, king of Egypt, asked him in secret to entreat God to reveal to him, by some miracle, which is the best religion.' Later legend asserted that Francis offered to walk through a fire to prove *106* the truth of his faith; but the Sultan prudently refused, and Francis's missionary work among the Muslims came to a speedy end.

Missionary work went on hand in hand with the Crusades: the eleventh century had seen the conversion of Scandinavia completed, together with that of Hungary and Poland; in the twelfth century large tracts of northern and central Europe were the scene of missionary enterprise. In the thirteenth century news began to trickle through of the Mongol empire of Jenghiz Khan, and the popes dreamed of a great act of missionary strategy which would encircle Islam. In the event this failed, and the Crusades and missionary enterprise tended to decay together, until the latter was revived in the days of the Counter-Reformation.

The meeting of St Francis and the Sultan is one of many ways in which the *poverello* can be seen to reflect and summarize the themes of this book. It is sometimes the most exceptional figures which help to bring a past age most vividly to life. We must not look to Francis for the actions or reactions of an ordinary man; but he will show us the interests and assumptions of his age softened and deepened by a rare humanity and illuminated by a brilliant imagination. His father was a merchant in a small Italian city; but a merchant with connections which took him into France, where he was travelling when Francis, 'Francesco', the Frank or Frenchman, was born in Assisi. Mercantile activity was developing the prosperity of Europe, and developing the capacity of cities small and large to cultivate the arts of war and peace. The rich young ruler in the Gospel went away sorrowing. Francis joyfully gave up all the wealth to which he had been brought up – joyfully, but not easily; his acute sense of what money could mean comes out in his almost violent insistence that his friars, vowed to poverty, should not touch or handle coins: the brother who pressed him to accept money to further some highly laudable cause was made to carry it in his teeth and drop it in a pile of manure, so that coins should always retain this association in his mind. Francis knew the subtlety of human temptation, and had a brilliant gift for direct teaching through the senses of smell and hearing and above all of sight: he acted many little parables before his friars. He also knew, from his father and probably from his own feelings as a boy, the power of money to attract and captivate. But his early ambitions had not lain in the market place. He had heard stories of chivalry and dreamed of being a knight; he had engaged in the petty warfare of the Italian cities and had been imprisoned in Perugia for his pains. He had used his father's money to buy arms and the trappings of chivalry, and had planned to join a band of *condottieri*. From

106 St Francis and the Sultan, from Giotto's fresco in the Bardi Chapel in Sta Croce, Florence. 'Command that a great fire be lit and I will enter it with your priests, to show you which faith is the more sure.' Thus St Bonaventure rendered Francis's challenge to the Sultan

this he was saved by a revulsion of feeling and a sudden illness, and by a growing sense that his call was to another of the many ideals of the age.

It was Francis's practice in later years, when he met a worm on the path or road on which he was walking, to pick it up carefully and place it on one side. A horror of seeing creatures trampled on and squashed was a conventional attribute of a medieval saint; but this was hardly the point in Francis's mind. The worm was a traditional symbol of the Saviour: 'I am a worm and no man' was interpreted as referring to Jesus Himself. Francis enforced the meaning of this paradox of humility by taking what would have been regarded as absurd pains to save a mere worm from its fate.

107 When he instructed the birds to sing God's praises he was not indulging in sentimental fantasy, but forcing on his hearers his conviction that the world was God's world, a part of the wonder of His creation. This was in tune with the beginning of a new tendency to look straight at nature and a new capacity to reproduce it with precision, which reaches its first perfection in the middle of the thirteenth century.

God's world – and so good, however perverted by the consequences of the Fall. The notion that the world was good needed some emphasis in an age and a land accustomed to the preaching of the Cathars, who taught that the world was irremediably evil. Cathar doctrine grew and flourished in western Europe in the twelfth and thirteenth centuries partly because it was attuned to a profound traditional attitude to God and the world: God was seen as a judge, the wickedness of the world was so far removed from his goodness that every human activity was tainted with sin and Jesus was thought of also as a judge – it was all but forgotten that he had once been a man. The Cathars, indeed, denied that he

107 St Francis preaching to the birds. Matthew Paris's drawing, 1236–50, one of the earliest surviving representations

had been a man: the Incarnation had only been an appearance, Jesus was a spirit in human form. But even while this doctrine enjoyed its greatest power, an interest in the human Jesus was also coming to appeal – and with it a renewed interest in the divine capacities of human nature, and (at the theological level) in human qualities. In a famous midnight gathering in Greccio, Francis united two of the most vital elements in his experience when he arranged for the Christmas Mass to be celebrated with all solemnity in an improvised stable with real donkeys and oxen standing by.

Communities of men dedicated to poverty were a familiar sight in France and Italy in Francis's childhood. Many of them, like the groups which gathered round Waldo (the Waldensians), the merchant of Lyons who had abandoned his wealth for a life of preaching and poverty, had started in orthodoxy and ended in heresy. But the principle of obedience to the Church's hierarchy was deep and strong in Francis, and this explains why he visited Pope and Curia as soon as his community began to form, and why he looked constantly in later years to Pope and Cardinal Protector, not to grant him privileges or special protection, but to help him to sustain the ideal of his Order within the established hierarchy of the Church. He made of obedience the central pillar of his Order; but it was no negative, passive obedience, but joyful submission.

'Holy obedience . . . makes a man subject to all men on this earth, and not to men only, but to the beasts of the field, to do with him – so far as is given to them from the Lord on high – what they will.'

Thus Francis added a new dimension to one of the most conventional and traditional principles of the society in which he lived. Similarly, there was nothing new in dedicating one's life to poverty; nor in the perception that there could be little direct contact between the hierarchy of the Church, authoritarian, powerful, rich, educated, and the ignorant poor masses of the people. But Francis found new methods of forming links between them, and made a new effort to give some unity or coherence to Christian society. The history of his Order and of the Church in the centuries after his death constantly gives evidence of his failure. But to say that Francis failed is, in the end, no more sensible than to say that Rembrandt failed as a painter because he died bankrupt.

'The brothers should rejoice', wrote Francis in one version of his *Rule*, 'when they are living among humble, despised folk, among the poor and weak, sick, lepers, beggars.' It needed emphasis: any success the friars might enjoy depended on their being accepted by the poor as of their own kind. Nor was it easy even for Francis. 'The Lord granted me to begin to do penance because, when I lived among my sins, it seemed to me too horrible even to look at lepers: and the Lord himself led me among them and I did a work of mercy with them. . . . And so what seemed horrible was transformed to sweetness both of mind and body. And after a little delay I left the life of the world. And the Lord gave me great faith in churches . . . and in priests. . . . And I wish above all that the most holy mysteries [of Christ's body and blood] shall be honoured, revered and kept in precious places. . . . And after the Lord gave me some brothers, no one showed me what I ought to do; but the Highest himself revealed to me that I ought to live according to the pattern of the Holy Gospel. And in few words and simply I had it written down, and the Lord Pope confirmed it to me. . . .'

7

Select Bibliography

General

For a general view of society in the eleventh and twelfth centuries:
SOUTHERN, R. W., *The Making of the Middle Ages*, London 1953.

Late Middle Ages

DU BOULAY, F. R. H., *An Age of Ambition*, London 1970, a very useful corrective to Huizinga and other studies of the nineteen-twenties and thirties, though confined to England.
HUIZINGA, J., *The Waning of the Middle Ages*, translated by F. Hopman, London 1924.

St Francis and the Franciscans

BROOKE, R. B., *Early Franciscan Government*, Cambridge 1959.
KNOWLES, D., *The Religious Orders in England*, I, Cambridge 1948.
SABATIER, P., *Vie de S. François d'Assise*, Paris 1893/4, translated by L. S. Houghton, London 1926.

The Papacy

BARRACLOUGH, G., *The Medieval Papacy*, London 1969.
ULLMANN, W., *The Growth of Papal Government in the Middle Ages*, London 1955.

Kingship

BROOKE, C., *The Saxon and Norman Kings*, London 1963.
FOLZ, R., *The Concept of Empire in Western Europe from the 5th to the 14th Century*, London 1969.
KERN, F., *Kingship, Law and the Constitution in the Middle Ages*, translated by S. B. Chrimes, Oxford 1939.

Lords and peasants

BLOCH, M., *Feudal Society*, translated by L. A. Manyon, London 1961.
—— *French Rural History*, translated by J. Sondheimer, London 1966.
DUBY, G., *Rural Economy and Country Life in the Medieval West*, translated by C. Postan, London 1968.
PAINTER, S., *Mediaeval Society*, Ithaca 1951.
TIERNEY, B., *Medieval Poor Law*, Berkeley and Los Angeles 1959.

Towns

BERESFORD, M. W., *New Towns of the Middle Ages*, London 1967.
LOBEL, M. D. (ed.), *Historic Towns*, I, London and Oxford 1969.
WALEY, D. P., *The Italian City Republics*, London 1969.

133

References

Quotations from Sabatier are from op. cit., English trans., p. xxxiii (slightly adapted); from Suger, my own translation from *Abbot Suger on the Abbey Church of St-Denis*, ed. E. Panofsky (Princeton 1946), p. 40, with Ezekiel, 28:13 in the Douai version as in ibid., pp. 62–63, and *Vie de Louis VI le Gros*, ed. H. Waquet (Paris 1929), *c.* 28, pp. 218 ff., 228; from the cardinals' letter in 1241, from K. Hampe's edition in *Sitzungsberichte der Heidelberg. Akad. der Wissenschaften*, phil.-hist. Klasse, 1913, pp. 3–34, esp. 27–30; from Jacques de Vitry, *Testimonia Minora Saeculi XIII de S. Francisco Assisiensi*, ed. L. Lemmens (Quaracchi 1926), p. 80; from St Francis, *Opuscula S. Francisci* (2 ed., Quaracchi 1941), pp. 21 (*Salutatio Virtutum*), 77–82 (*Testament*). Except where specified these are in my own translation (for the rest of St Francis' works, there is a complete translation in L. Sherley-Price, *St Francis of Assisi*, London 1959). The account of Stratford-upon-Avon is based on E. M. Carus-Wilson, 'The first half-century of the Borough of Stratford-upon-Avon', *Economic History Review*, 2nd Series, XVIII (1965), 46–63.

List of Illustrations

19 *St Clare mourning St Francis*; fresco attributed to Giotto in the Upper Church of S Francesco, Assisi, end thirteenth century. Photo *Marzari*

20 Watercolour of the third church at Cluny, interior, looking east. J.-B. Lallemand, *c.* 1773. Photo *Courtauld Institute*

21 Beasts in relief at Beaulieu (Corrèze), early twelfth century. Photo *Jean Roubier*

22 Fontenay abbey church, interior, looking east. Photo *Monuments Historiques*

23 Abbot Suger; detail from a stained glass window in St-Denis abbey church; mid-twelfth century, reset in the fourteenth-century window of the Life of the Virgin. Photo *Jean Roubier*. For 23–27 see E. Panofsky, *Abbot Suger on the abbey church of St-Denis* (Princeton 1946)

24 Roman porphyry vase with gold mount in the shape of an eagle, made for Abbot Suger; from St-Denis, mount *c.* 1140. Louvre, Paris. Photo *Connaissance des Arts*

25 Sardonyx chalice mounted in gold, made for Abbot Suger; from St-Denis, *c.* 1140. *National Gallery of Art, Washington D.C. Widener Collection*

26 St-Denis, Suger's ambulatory (1140–44). Photo *Courtauld Institute of Art*

27 Detail of a diptych leaf, *The Mass of St Giles*; Flemish, by the Master of St Giles, *c.* 1495. By courtesy of the Trustees of the National Gallery, London. Photo *John Webb*. On this picture see W. M. Hinkle in *Journ. of the Warburg and Courtauld Inst.*, XXVIII (1965), 110 ff.

28 Shrine and royal tombs in the Chapel of Edward the Confessor, Westminster Abbey, London, thirteenth–fifteenth centuries. Photo *National Monuments Record*

29 Tomb of Henry III, Westminster Abbey, late thirteenth century. Photo *National Monuments Record*

30 Tomb of Edward III, Westminster Abbey, late fourteenth century. Photo *Royal Commission on Historical Monuments*

31 Seal of the City of London, thirteenth century. Photo *British Museum*. See W. de G. Birch, *Catalogue of Seals in the . . . Brit. Mus.*, II (1892), pp. 107–8, no. 5068

32 Miniature from a *Coronation Order*, the coronation ceremony; ?French, early fourteenth century. MS. 20, f. 68. *By permission of the Master and Fellows of Corpus Christi College, Cambridge*

33 Miniature of the anointing and coronation of Edward the Confessor, from the mid thirteenth-century MS. of Matthew Paris's *La estoire de Seint Aedward le rei* (not from the author's hand), Cambridge University Library MS. Ee. iii. 59, f. 9. Photo *Cambridge University Library*. See R. Vaughan, *Matthew Paris* (Cambridge 1958), pp. 168 ff., 221–22

34 Coronation Chair made for Edward I, containing the Stone of Scone, 1300. London, Westminster Abbey

35 The Holy Lance, Vienna, Weltliche Schatzkammer. On this and other regalia, see P. E. Schramm, *Herrschaftszeichen und Staatssymbolik* (Stuttgart 1954–56), II, pp. 492–537; pl. 72 a–e

36 The Imperial Crown of Otto I (936–73), with bow added in the time of Conrad II (1024–39). Vienna, Weltliche Schatzkammer. Photo *Erwin Meyer*. See Schramm, op. cit., II, esp. pls. 85 ff.

37 A king's nightmare; Henry I of England (1100–35) dreams that he is threatened by the three orders of the kingdom. English miniature, mid-twelfth century. Oxford, Bodleian Library, Corpus Christi Coll. MS. 157, pp. 382–83. Photo *Bodleian Library, with the permission of the President and Fellows of Corpus Christi College, Oxford*

38 Equestrian aquamanile, *c.* 1300. Photo *British Museum*

39 Relief of an armed knight, probably twelfth century, from the Church of Notre Dame de la Règle, Limoges. Photo *Musée Municipal, Limoges*

40 Archer in knight's armour, from the Bayeux Tapestry; see Phaidon ed., pl. 61, cf. p. 174. Photo *Giraudon*, reproduced with the permission of *La Ville de Bayeux*

41 Pope Boniface VIII presides over a consistory; detail of miniature from the Sext (Decretals of Boniface VIII), Brit. Mus. Addit. MS. 23923, f. 2 (late fourteenth century: see *Catalogue of Additions to the MSS. in the British Museum, 1854–60* (1875), p. 918). Photo courtesy the *Trustees of the British Museum*

42 Pipe Roll of Henry I. London, Public Record Office E372 Pipe Roll 1. From the section relating to Notts and Derbyshire (ed. J. Hunter, p. 8). Photo *Public Record Office*; Crown Copyright reserved

43 Silver and gold coins; silver pennies of William I (pax type), Henry III (short cross), Henry III (showing long cross); and gold penny of Henry III (see G.C. Brooke, *English Coins*, London 1932, pp. 83, 110–12, pls. XVIII, XXII). Photo *P. Clayton*

44 Chaucer's Parson; from the Ellesmere MS. of the *Canterbury Tales*, now in Henry E. Huntington Library, San Marino, California. Photo *Huntington Library*

45 Gilt copper plaque decorated with champlevé enamel, showing Henry of Blois, Bishop of Winchester, kneeling and holding what is probably a reliquary; English (Winchester), mid-twelfth century. Photo courtesy the *Trustees of the British Museum*

46 Winchester Cathedral; treasury in south transept, mid-twelfth century. Photo *Courtauld Institute*

47 Winchester, Wolvesey Castle, mainly mid-twelfth century (from 1138). Photo *Tessa Ward*

48 Glastonbury Abbey from the air. Photo *J.K.S. St Joseph* (Crown Copyright reserved): see D. Knowles and St Joseph, *Monastic Sites from the Air* (Cambridge 1952), p. 29

49 The Emperor Henry VI; from the Minnesinger Codex, *c.* 1315. Heidelberg, Manessischen Liederhandschrift MS. Pal. germ. 848. Photo *Universitätsbibliothek, Heidelberg*

50 The Emperor Frederick II; from an early MS. of his own treatise on falconry, thirteenth century. Vatican Library, cod. Pal. Lat. 1071, f. IV. Photo *Biblioteca Apostolica Vaticana*

51 Miniature from the *Cronaca Villani*; election of Pope John XXII; Italian, second half of fourteenth century. Vatican Library, cod. Chigi L. viii. 296, f. 214v. Photo *Biblioteca Apostolica Vaticana*

52 Miniature from the *Cronaca Villani*; coronation of Pope Clement VI in the presence of King Philip of France, King Charles de Valois of Naples, and barons; Italian, second half of fourteenth century. MS. as above, f. 186v. Photo *Biblioteca Apostolica Vaticana*

53 The Angevin Empire; map drawn by David Eccles, with hatchings to show the stages in its growth

54 Lady Margaret Beaufort, mother of Henry VII; from a late fifteenth-century panel, artist unknown. London, National Portrait Gallery. Photo *National Portrait Gallery*

55 Henry VII; from his effigy by Torrigiani, London, Westminster Abbey. Photo *Warburg Institute*

56 The parable of the Labourers in the Vineyard; from the Codex Aureus Epternacensis, eleventh century, Nürnberg, Germanisches National-Museum, MS 1138, f. 76v; see *Golden Gospels of Echternach*, ed. P. Metz, (London, 1957), pl. 67. Photo *Germanisches National-Museum*

57 The grape-harvest; from an English miseri-cord, mid-fourteenth century, Gloucester Cathedral. Photo *Edwin Smith*. See G.L. Remnant, *A Catalogue of Misericords in Great Britain* (Oxford 1969), p. 51, no. 51

58 Harrowing and sowing the winter corn; from a scene representing October in a calendar in stained glass of the early six-teenth century. Victoria and Albert Museum, roundel from Cassiobury Park. Photo *Victoria and Albert Museum*, Crown Copyright reserved

59 Padbury (Bucks), showing corrugated pas-ture representing medieval strips, from the air. Photo *J.K.S. St Joseph*, Crown Copy-right reserved. See M.W. Beresford and St Joseph, *Medieval England; an Aerial Survey* (Cambridge 1958), pp. 30–33

60 Country life in France, outside the walls of Paris, showing the Ile de la Cité, Sainte-Chapelle and royal palace; from the *Très Riches Heures du duc de Berry*, by the Limbourg brothers, 1413–16. Chantilly, Musée Condé, MS. 65, f. 6v. Photo *Giraudon*

61 Peasants at work (actually Israelites in Egypt), from an English MS. of the eleventh century, second quarter: British Museum, Cotton MS. Claudius B. iv, f. 79v (Ælfric's paraphrase of *Pentateuch* and *Joshua*). Photo courtesy the *Trustees of the British Museum*. See F. Wormald, *English Drawings of the tenth and eleventh centuries* (London 1952), pp. 39 ff., 67

62 Terraces in the Apennines; vineyards in the Cinqueterre, near Genoa. Photo *Emily Lane*

63 The traces of a lost village; Burston (Bucks), from the air. Photo *J.K.S. St Joseph*, Crown Copyright reserved. See *Medieval England* (cit. pl. 59), pp. 115–16

64 Meadows on the Etzel-Pass, Canton Schwyz, showing the Meinradskapelle (originally of the thirteenth century, later much altered), near the Sihlsee. Photo *Swiss National Tourist Office*

65 Summer pasture and forest just below the Klausenpass, Canton Uri. Photo *Swiss National Tourist Office*. The frontier be-tween Uri and Glarus has always lain some distance east of the pass, which shows that the men of the Canton valued the uplands and used the pass in the Middle Ages. The frontier is based on a boundary established in an agreement attributed to the end of the twelfth century.

66 The Etruscan Gate at Perugia, with Roman arch and Renaissance loggia. Photo *Mansell Collection*

67 Florence in the late fifteenth century, from an engraving of 1486–90 (see F. Lippman, *Art of Wood Engraving in Fifteenth Century Italy*, London, 1888, pp. 30ff., 72–73). Photo *J.R. Freeman*

68 The Wrekin, surmounted by prehistoric hill-fort and town. Photo *British Tourist Authority*

69, 70 Viriconium (Wroxeter) and Shrews-bury. Photos *J.K.S. St Joseph*, Crown Copy-right reserved

71 Trier. Inset view from an eighteenth-century map, inscribed 'M. Seutter, Trier an der Mosel, 1737'. British Museum, Map Room. Photo courtesy the *Trustees of the British Museum*

72 La Bastide d'Armagnac. Photo *Institut Géo-graphique National*

73 Alnmouth, a new town of the twelfth century, from the air. Photo *J.K.S. St Joseph*, Crown Copyright reserved. See *Medieval England* (cit. pl. 59), pp. 190–92

74 Durham from the air. Photo *J.K.S. St Joseph*, Crown Copyright reserved. See *Medieval England*, pp. 183–85.

75 A fifteenth-century town, with booths and stalls; from the Statutes of the Drapers of Bologna, 1411. Bologna, Museo Civico. Photo *Archivio Fotografico d'Arte, A. Villani e Figli, Bologna*

138

76 Spoleto, from the north, showing the Rocca and Aqueduct. Photo *Mansell Collection*

77 Spoleto, from an old engraving

78 Assisi, from a sixteenth-century engraving – 'Assisi nell'Umbria, patr. di S. Francesco', ?1590. British Museum Map Room. Photo courtesy the *Trustees of the British Museum*

79 Assisi, street scene. Photo *Leonard von Matt*. See L. von Matt and W. Hauser, *St Francis of Assisi* (London 1956), pl. 43

80 Old Sarum; the Norman castle and cathedral within the prehistoric ramparts, from the air. Photo *J.K.S. St Joseph*, Crown Copyright reserved. See *Medieval England* (cit. pl. 59), pp. 185–87

81 A lofty *torre* in Perugia. Photo *Mansell Collection*

82 The Shambles in York, from a photograph taken between 1902 and 1910. Photo *National Monuments Record*

83 The quarters of Palermo, from a panorama of 1195–96: Bern, Burgerbibliothek, MS. 120/II, f. 98 – Petrus de Ebulo, *Liber ad Honorem Augusti*. See *Schätze der Burgerbibliothek, Bern* (Bern 1953), pp. 120–23

84 Detail of *Good Government*, fresco by Ambrogio Lorenzetti, personification of Siena and the Virtues; 1337–39. Palazzo Publico, Siena. Photo *Scala*. See N. Rubinstein in *Journ. of the Warburg and Courtauld Inst.*, XXI (1958), pp. 179–209

85 Another detail from the same fresco showing the fruits of peace and good order. Photo *Scala*

86 Conisborough (Yorkshire), an English baronial keep of the twelfth century. Photo *National Monuments Record*. On castles, see W. Anderson and W. Swaan, *Castles of Europe* (London 1970); R. A. Brown, *English Medieval Castles* (London 1954); T. S. R. Boase, *Kingdoms and strongholds of the Crusaders* (London 1971).

87 Ludlow Castle across the river Teme; eleventh-century walls surmounted by fourteenth-century towers. Photo *National Monuments Record*

88 The Norman motte or mound being built, from the Bayeux Tapestry (late eleventh century). See Phaidon ed., pl. 51 and p. 172; *Hestengaceastra = Hastings*

89 Berkhamsted; the castle from the air. Photo *J.K.S. St Joseph*, Crown Copyright reserved

90 Angers Castle; rebuilt in the thirteenth century after the French conquest of Anjou from the English. Photo *Monuments Historiques*

91 Kerak, a great crusading castle of the twelfth century. Photo *A.F. Kersting*. See Boase, p. 79

92 Miniature from the *Chroniques de France et de Saint Denis*; St Louis leaving on the Seventh Crusade; French, early fourteenth century. British Museum, Royal MS. 16.G. VI, f. 404v. Photo courtesy the *Trustees of the British Museum*

93 Miniature from the *Descriptio Terrae Sanctae* of Burchardus Theutonicus, the siege of Jerusalem; Italian, late thirteenth century. Padua, Biblioteca del Seminario, MS. 74, f. 13v. Photo *Biblioteca del Seminario*

94 St James as crusader, from twelfth-century tympanum of Compostela Cathedral. Photo *MAS, Barcelona*

95 St James in pilgrim costume; late fifteenth-century statue of painted stone at Semur-en-Auxois, Côte d'Or; now in the Louvre. Photo *Louvre*

96 Santiago de Compostela Cathedral, nave of the early twelfth century. Photo *MAS, Barcelona*

97 Christ as pilgrim, with staff and cockle, on the road to Emmaus, but dressed as for the road to Santiago. Eleventh-century relief

in cloister at S. Domingo de Silos, Spain. Photo G. *Zarnecki*

98 The return from Santiago; pilgrims playing games to shorten the journey. From the fifteenth-century *Hours of the Duchess of Burgundy*, French. Chantilly, Musée Condé, MS. 76, f. 9. Photo *Giraudon*

99–103 A group of late medieval pilgrim tokens, fourteenth–fifteenth century. British Museum. Photo courtesy the *Trustees of the British Museum*

104 Cambridge, Church of the Holy Sepulchre, early twelfth century. Photo *Royal Commission on Historical Monuments*, Crown Copyright reserved

105 Jews suffering persecution; the expulsion from England in 1290, from an English MS. (*Flores Historiarum*) of the early fourteenth century. British Museum, Cotton MS. Nero D. ii, f. 183v. Photo courtesy the *Trustees of the British Museum*

106 *St Francis and the Sultan*, from Giotto's fresco in the Bardi Chapel in Sta Croce, Florence; perhaps *c.* 1320, Photo *Scala*

107 St Francis preaching to the birds; Matthew Paris's drawing 1236–50, one of the earliest surviving representations. Corpus Christi College, Cambridge, MS. 16, f. 66. Photo *Courtauld Institute*. Reproduced with permission of the *Master and Fellows of Corpus Christi College*. See A. G. Little in *Collectanea Franciscana*, 1 (Brit. Soc. of Franciscan Studies, 1914), pp. 1 ff.; R. Vaughan, *Matthew Paris* (Cambridge 1958), Chapter XI

Index

Page numbers in italics refer to illustrations